Date Due

Bayfield	JUN 0 3 2000	
ILLO	JUL 0 8 2000	
ILLO	0002 8 0 JUL	
BAY Nov 2	JUL 0 8 2000	
JAN 2 2 1983		
MAR 5 1983		
NOV 2 1983		
AUG 1 8		
JUL - 2 1986		
SEP 7 1988		
DEC 14		
DEC 2 8 1988		

LADY RANCHER

LADY RANCHER

BY

GERTRUDE MINOR ROGER

Hancock House Publishers Inc.

ISBN 0-88839-038-6

Copyright © 1979 Gertrude Minor Roger

Cataloging in Publication Data

Roger, Gertrude Minor.
Lady rancher

1. Roger, Gertrude Minor. 2. Ranch
life - Saskatchewan. 3. Ranch life -
British Columbia. 4. Ranchers -
Saskatchewan - Biography. 5. Ranchers -
British Columbia - Biography. I. Title.
FC3525.1.R64A3   971.24'3'030924
F1072.R64A3   C79-091136-1
          ISBN 0-88839-038-6

Published simultaneously in Canada and the United States by:

 HANCOCK HOUSE PUBLISHERS LTD.
3215 Island View Road   SAANICHTON, B.C. V0S 1M0

HANCOCK HOUSE PUBLISHERS INC.
12008 1st Avenue South   SEATTLE, WA. 98168

Photo credit for cover:
British Columbia Government Photograph.

Contents

In
loving memory
of
John.

ACKNOWLEDGEMENTS

I would like to thank my cousin Jean for helping me get this book off the ground and my daughter Janet, who did the typing.

My appreciation also to Cliff Faulkner, well-known Canadian author, for his valuable help.

Finally, a special thanks to publisher David Hancock and editor Robert Sward.

Chapter I:

Taking Stock

Everything has to begin sometime. My ranching career began at five o'clock one morning in July, 1944, at the old *age 18* Cruikshank Ranch near Beechy, Saskatchewan. The ranch belonged to John and Harry Minor, who both owned other ranches as well. John's other ranch was across the meandering South Saskatchewan River in the Great Sandhills country and Harry's was near Medicine Hat, Alberta. This ranch was called the Cruikshank Ranch because when a western rancher buys up another man's holdings, he generally keeps calling his place by its original name. He knows that people will go on using it anyhow. To a greenhorn like me, all this was pretty confusing.

"Be sure you work," young John Minor whispered as we were getting up from the breakfast table. "Pop has no use for anyone who just stands around." I nodded groggily, thinking of the warm bed I had been forced to leave when Aunt Flora—Harry Minor's wife—had prodded me awake at what seemed like the middle of the night. But I knew about John's father, and I was really afraid of him. All my life I had heard about his gruffness, roughness and his endless cussing. And this was branding time—as good an excuse for cussing as you're likely to find. Branding amounts to a sort of rangeland inventory—the time when a cattleman takes stock of all the critters on his place and puts his special mark on any newcomers. Everybody is expected to pull his weight at a branding.

Looking up, I caught the old man's piercing blue eyes on me and instinctively straightened like a sagging rookie under the baleful glance of his top sergeant.

It was the first time I had ever had anything to do with

cattle ranching. I had been raised on a grain farm close to the town of Abbey near the Great Sandhills. The only cattle we had owned were a handful of placid dairy cows. But I had always known about the Minors who were a big pioneer ranching family. I met young John when he started attending Roe High School three miles from our farm. He was the best looking boy in our class and so full of energy it seemed to be bursting out of him.

When John asked me to come to the Cruikshank Ranch for two days while they branded the spring calves, I jumped at the chance. An invitation like that has a special meaning in cattle country. It means that a girl is being "sized up" to see if she is good enough to ride with the outfit. I knew what was running through Pop Minor's mind as he looked at me. "John seems a bit stuck on this girl," he was thinking. "Is she a 'good doer' or isn't she?" In cattle talk, a 'good doer' is a critter that will perform well on a minimum amount of feed.

Then the men began to file out of the kitchen, and John's father went with them. Thankfully, I stayed behind. This was the place I could be most help, I told myself. After all, I was eighteen and I knew something about cooking. I had baked a cake once or twice—and I could boil water.

The kitchen was warm with the heat of the oven where a large roast of beef had been sizzling since three a.m. Aunt Flora, and Mrs. Allan, the wife of ranch foreman Dooley Allan, had been up early preparing food for the crew of fifty men. But as soon as I saw the way those two women were turning out pies—a dozen at a time it seemed—I knew I would be of little use to them.

"Anything I can do to help?" I asked half-heartedly, hoping the answer would be in the negative. It was. With great relief I hurried out of the kitchen and headed toward the corral. At least out here I could watch the action without feeling so completely useless. Nobody would expect a girl to help with the branding—that was man's work.

I climbed up onto the corral fence and settled myself as comfortably as possible. The air was cool and still and the sun had begun to inch its way up over the horizon.

Below, in the corral, the restless cattle were milling around the branding fire, stirring up the brown dust. Separated from their calves during the roundup, the cows were bawling loudly as they searched for them. The little ones answered plaintively. Every once in a while a cow and her calf would find each other for a moment, and the calf would have time for a couple of quick sucks before being pushed along by the anxious herd.

Near the corral fence, where the horses were tied, John and his cousin, Dode, were tightening their saddle cinches and coiling their ropes. They were going to do the roping. Their job was to ride into the herd and toss a rope, catch the calf by the hind feet and drag the kicking, struggling young critter to the branding fire. A couple of cowboys were hauling old fence posts to a pile beside the fire so there would be lots of fuel when needed. John's sister, Helen, was busy filling a syringe with vaccine so the calves could be innoculated for a deadly disease called "Blackleg." Putting the last branding iron carefully into the bright flames was Harry Minor, and I winced for the tender hides that would feel the bite of the hot metal. The male calves had even worse indignities awaiting them.

But the man I had my eye on was Pop Minor, hoping at the same time that I would escape his. For here I was sitting idly while everyone else was working. Shoulders well back, belly out, and chest thrust forward, he walked briskly around the corral bellowing orders. Everytime he boomed a command, a stream of cuss words came pouring out with it. Half in fear, half in awe, I followed the progress of his dilapidated Stetson as he moved among the horses, not realizing what the bellowing really meant—that the old man was enjoying himself immensely.

"You gonna rope off that son-of-a-bitchin' horse?" he roared at John as he came up to his eighteen-year-old son.

"Why not? He needs the practice."

"He's a crazy bastard, that's why! And you'll get your goddam neck broke!"

John grinned and paid no attention to his father. The latter stomped off whistling cheerfully, happy in the thought that he had given a paternal warning but proud that his son had "guts."

Next, Pop planted his short, thickset body beside the fire and took a worn whetstone out of his shirt pocket. Then he delved into his righthand pants pocket for a knife. He flipped the blade open and tested the edge with a blunt calloused thumb. Spitting on the stone, he began to work the blade deftly back and forth across its smooth face.

His brother and partner, Harry Minor, was circling the fire, checking the branding irons. When he lifted one out to look at it, I could see that the business end shone with a cherry-red glow. As the two bosses worked, they spat choppy phrases at each other, masking their mutual affection in gruff remarks—some of which bordered on insult. Pop honed away at his blade until his educated thumb told him it was sharp enough. Then knife and stone disappeared into their respective pockets.

"That should do the son-of-a-bitch," he said with some satisfaction. What it would do, and to whom, I was soon to find out.

"Come on, let's get going!" His voice boomed out so suddenly I almost fell off the fence. "Half the morning's gone already."

Still shouting at the top of his lungs, he went on to brag that in his younger days everybody got up earlier, could mount quicker, ride harder, and work their ropes faster than anybody present.

I saw John grinning to himself as he reached for the reins of his horse and swung easily up into the saddle. All in the course of the same graceful movement, he and his horse began to move in on the milling herd. Suddenly his rope twirled out and caught a darting calf by its two hind feet. Tightening the rope and spinning his horse at the same time, John hauled the bawling critter toward the fire where a couple of calf wrestlers waited. They grabbed their victim quickly—one at its head and the other at its hind legs. Then they slipped the rope free so that John could go back for another animal.

I don't know about those supermen of the Old West, but my guess is that none of them could have done it any better. For one thing, there was a brief glint of pride in Pop's eyes which spoke volumes.

At that moment Dode came riding in dragging another calf. Another hand, Neil Clarey, stood tensed ready to wrestle it. Neil grabbed one front leg and tugged hard, but the wirey calf refused to go down. He tugged again. This time, the calf sprawled on its side, but so did Neil. The struggle degenerated into a seesaw. Desperately, Neil glanced around the corral, looking for a partner. I looked, too, but nobody was available. The calf struggled to its feet again. Silently I cheered.

"Hey! Come and help me wrestle!" Neil shouted over his shoulder.

I looked around to see whom he was yelling at, but couldn't see anybody.

"Hey you! Come and give me a hand here!" he repeated. He seemed to be looking my way. But that was impossible.

"You mean me?" I choked weakly.

"Yes, you!" he said with a grin.

This is ridiculous, I thought wildly, as I slid gingerly off the fence into the danger of the corral. I couldn't wrestle a calf! What will I do? I thought desperately.

"Here, grab a leg!" Neil instructed, nodding at the critter's top hind leg which was flailing the air. I grabbed the leg and gave a little tug on it. The calf reacted with a well-aimed kick which sent my light body spinning across the dusty corral floor, rear end down, into a mass of gooey fresh manure. I could feel that awful wetness oozing through the seat of my pants as I squirmed around trying to get up without having to sink my hands in it.

Now, both the calf and I were ready for a fight to the finish. Neil was thrown around the animal's plunging head, while Dode was trying to keep pressure on the rope so the calf wouldn't get away. Whenever I maneuvered myself so I could make a grab for a leg, the calf kicked his roped leg violently. I grabbed at anything I could get hold of, but with very little success. Finally, I got a firm grip on the critter's free hind leg, threw my weight against his rear and he went down with a thud. With me still bobbing wildly around, the branding crew went to work.

First came Helen, John's sister, who quickly jabbed her needle under the calf's left front leg. At the same time, one of the men planted a glowing branding iron on the calf's exposed flank. The calf bellowed with pain, and a sudden puff of smoke rose from the burning hair. It stung my eyes, and the smell nauseated me so that I turned my face in against my shoulder to get away from it. Then I looked up to see Pop moving in with his razor-sharp knife.

That's when I learned that steers are made, not born. To my horror, he began to castrate the squirming animal. Blood trickled freely, and my stomach churned and churned. I became acutely embarrassed that I should be watching this rangeland ritual with all these men standing around.

"Bring me that bucket!" yelled Pop, and for once he was not just exercising his tonsils. When a young boy ran over with the blood spattered testicle pail, I could see it already contained a bloody mess of the things, which meant that John's branding team had not been loafing on the job. Although I tried not to stare at these grisly contents, I seemed unable to pull my eyes away. I assumed the testicles were to be fed to the dogs, and it disgusted me. Surely their dogs deserved something better than this!

But there was more blood-letting to come, and I still had my ringside seat right beside the action. Pop turned toward us again, bent laboriously over the bawling animal's head and with one quick stroke sliced off the tip of an ear to earmark it. As the blood trickled down the little white face I could feel the blood leaving mine. Then suddenly the struggle was over, and the wounded calf was released to scamper back into the safety of the herd.

I heard the anguished bellow of another calf, and I looked around in a panic. Dode was riding up through the dust with a second victim dragging behind his horse. "Surely, I don't have to do it all again." I groaned to myself. But I was wrong. I would have to do it over and over and over again.

"Grab him!" Neil shouted as he seized one front leg so he could flip the struggling calf. Dode kept his horse straining back to keep the rope tight. Not knowing what to do, I grabbed the critter's tail and sat down with a thud on the ground. Next I made a grab for the legs. Meanwhile, Dode was waiting impatiently for me to free his rope so he could go for another calf. With all the instructions being yelled at me, I was becoming more and more confused.

Just when I was about to give up, John rode over. Grinning broadly, he threw his leg over his horse's back and stepped down to the ground.

"You gotta have a system," he explained.

I didn't see how anybody could work out a system for anything as unpredictable as a frightened calf. But I got up so that John could show me how it should be done.

"Like this," he said, as he seized the calf's top leg, put one foot on the hock of the bottom leg, and sat down, jamming his other foot against the startled critter's rump as he did so. The calf gave up the struggle at once. It sure looked easy when John did it.

"Now you try it," he smiled.

I sat down and tried to duplicate John's quick, efficient movements. The calf made a half-hearted bid for freedom when it saw who was doing the pulling, but then it submitted to the inevitable. John slipped the rope off its hooves, and he and Dode rode back to the herd, chuckling.

Neil and I handled the next few calves with little difficulty. I found the job much easier now that I had a system. When the branding was about half over, everybody stopped for a break. Up to the fire came two men carrying a big tub full of bottled beer. They set it down by the fire and started handing out the refreshments.

With all the other smells I had encountered that day, I hated the thought of beer. I had never even tasted the stuff, but it's a familiar smell around any prairie town on a Saturday night, and I always thought anyone who would drink it was a sinner. Someone opened a bottle and thrust it toward me. Although my throat was parched, I shook my head. I would have loved a glass of cool, clear water, as the song says, but beer was the only liquid available.

"No thanks, I'm not thirsty," I lied, trying to work up enough saliva so I could swallow. Early training dies hard, I guess.

At last the branding was over, and the cows and their calves were turned loose. The ropers rode out with them for awhile to see that they got settled down, and that all the calves found their mothers. In the empty corral, the fetid smell of burning hair still hung in the air. Someone was dousing the fire. It hissed angrily, puffing out great clouds of smoke. While Pop Minor was helping his brother Harry pick up and store the branding irons, the rest of the men stood around joking and laughing after their hard morning's work.

Suddenly I felt very conspicuous as I stood there alone near the corral fence. I knew that I looked a mess. Blood and manure were splattered all over my shoes, socks, shirt, jeans and a large bruise on my left arm was already turning black and blue. Full of gritty brown dust, my hair hung in unsightly strings around my shoulders.

My person had fared about as well as my clothes. My eyes stung from the acrid smoke and the dust, my lips were chapped and my throat was parched. As I started walking toward the corral gate, my knees suddenly felt weak and I knew how tired I was. Slowly I opened the gate and stepped outside, keeping my eyes on the ground so I wouldn't have to look at any of the men who stood around the dying fire. I had an idea that some of those laughs were at my expense.

After I got cleaned up, John joined me and we walked over to the big tent which had been set up in front of the house as a sort of extra dining room.

"Say, you did great!" he smiled, giving me a friendly shove.

I smiled back gratefully, but thought to myself: "I may have pleased you, but I wonder what your father thinks?" One thing sure, my calf-wrestling skill would never call forth that glint of pride he had shown when he had watched his son rope a calf that morning.

Inside the tent, the fruit of Aunt Flora's and Mrs. Allan's early kitchen labors lay spread out on a long wooden table. A noisy crowd of men and women were lined up around it, filling their plates. I hesitated just inside the door, watching the others dig into the platters of steaming food. John nudged me toward the end of the line.

Then Pop's voice boomed out suddenly. "Here! Get that girl some food. She worked damned hard today!"

I flushed and hurriedly grabbed a plate. But inside I felt a warm glow of pleasure.

Breakfast was at six o'clock next morning. That's what range folks call "sleeping in." As I sat down beside John, people started passing around large platters of meat, eggs, hotcakes, toast. From one platter, John unloaded a pile of what looked like small, crispy-brown skinless sausages. They looked pretty good, although I had never been very strong on sausage meat for breakfast.

"Have some," he said, handing me the platter. For some reason everybody had stopped eating and was looking my way.

"What are they?" I whispered, with a hint of suspicion.

"Calf fries. Try some, you'll like 'em."

Suddenly I recalled a scene from the night before, when I had wandered past a couple of men working over a bucket. I remembered one of the men jokingly referring to something he called "prairie oysters." Now, in a flash, I realized why that bucket had seemed somehow familiar; only the blood was missing. That had been the calf testicle pail, and those men had been removing the outer skin and placing the meat into a pan.

In my horror, I almost dropped the platter. John took my hesitation as his cue to explain that calf fries are a much soughtafter delicacy.

"They're very tasty," he told me. "Go ahead, fill your plate."

"No thanks," I said hastily. "I'm really not very hungry."

"TRY SOME, GIRL!" Pop bellowed from one end of the long table. "THEY'RE REAL GOOD!"

Some of the faces watching us broke into broad grins. Even the more polite ones seemed to be struggling to hide their amusement.

I shook my head and passed the platter. Everybody on down the line heaped his plate with the things. The platter was empty in no time. But to me, eating part of an animal, especially that part, when the rest of it was still running around in the field was akin to cannibalism. Even though I wanted everybody to approve of me, I could not go that far. All of a sudden I had lost my appetite.

After breakfast, John and I loaded our things into his old De Soto and headed down the long, dusty road. Branding at the Cruikshank place was over and we were going home, John to his father's ranch southwest of Abbey, and I to my father's farm.

It was a cool, beautiful morning. Fleets of fluffy cumulus clouds moved slowly across the sky like stately Spanish galleons, and our spirits rode with them. As we sailed along the road with the dust rolling up behind us, the wind ruffled John's dark brown hair. He was smiling that crinkly smile of his and I was smiling, too. The night before he had asked me to marry him.

Chapter II:

Miracles Do Happen

I was sure there was no way we could get my father's consent to our marriage. Both John and I were just eighteen, and I knew Dad was pretty keen on my starting nurse's training in the fall, as we had planned earlier. Of his four daughters, I was the only one still at home and he was determined that I should "make something" of myself. The trouble was we would need his consent before we could even get a license, and we would need it in writing.

That's why I was wandering nervously about our yard like a yearling with shipping fever, listening for the sound of John's old De Soto rattling down the dirt road which led to our farm. For this was the night I planned to make myself Mrs. John Minor, and I hadn't even gotten around to telling my father! Ever since I had finished the supper dishes, I had wandered around trying to decide how I should go about it.

It was almost dark when I heard the car. I rushed around to the front so that I could catch John before he started banging on the door. He rolled down the side window and smiled at me.

"Oh John," I whispered, "it'll take a miracle."

"You mean you asked him?"

I shook my head. "I meant to, but everytime I started, my throat seemed to dry up."

"Are you all packed?"

"I've been ready for hours," I told him.

"Well, here goes," he laughed, as he slid out from behind the wheel. "One miracle coming up."

I'll wait here and let you talk to him," I said.

"If anything happens you can notify my next of kin," he nodded with a twinkle in his eye.

This brought another worry. His next of kin was rough, tough Pop Minor, and we would have to have his consent in writing, too. That meant we would need *two* miracles.

As I watched John stride confidently toward the house I kept my fingers crossed. If anyone could do it, he could, I thought.

My father had never intended to come to Canada. After he obtained his civil-engineering degree in Edinburgh, Scotland, he studied Spanish, planning to go to South America to help manage his uncle's OXO plant there. Just before he was ready to set sail, his father and uncle quarreled, so Dad came to Canada instead where he met and married my mother who was a music teacher. Lured to the rolling Prairies by tales about the opening of the West, they took up a homestead near Abbey, Saskatchewan. There was nothing in their genteel backgrounds to prepare them for the harsh realities of Prairie pioneering. Suddenly, in December 1926, mother died, leaving Dad to raise four daughters.

Dad was determined that we should get as much schooling as possible. Most of the world's troubles, he used to say, were the result of a lack of education. I was only nine months old when Mother died, so I spent the next five years with relatives and friends. But when I was five, I came back home to start school and my eldest sister, Evelyn, took over most of the responsibility of raising me.

All four of us were expected to help Dad run the farm. We did every job that he wanted done, and still made the three-mile trip to school with the horse and buggy every weekday so we could get the education he was always preaching about. The only pleasures he approved of were playing the piano and listening to our Marconi battery radio. He censored the latter so we wouldn't be contaminated. We were allowed to listen to the news, quiz programs and the Saturday night hockey game only. At any mention of the word love, Dad would snap off the set and give us a little lecture about wasting our time on something that did not increase our knowledge. "Education is the key to life," he would conclude. And he didn't mean sex education, either.

All this was running through my mind as I paced the yard in the moonlight waiting for John. I expect I felt a little guilty, too, for springing this on Dad with so little warning.

As I watched the door, I half expected to see John make a hasty exit on the toe of Dad's boot. When it finally did open, John bounded out with a wide grin on his face and triumphantly waved a piece of paper. On it, penned in Dad's formal boarding school script, was his consent for us to marry. Only one more miracle to go!

I wanted to rush in and thank Dad, and tell him that everything would be all right—that it would work out just fine. But something held me back. I guess I was afraid that he might change his mind. Stilling my qualms, I grabbed my suitcases from their hiding place in a clump of carragana bush and jumped into the car beside John. We tore out of the yard in a cloud of dust and smoke.

At the Minor house I chickened out again. I stayed in the den while John went in to talk to his father. John's mother had passed away when he was twelve. Pop was asleep in an adjoining bedroom.

"Pop!" I heard John say. "Are you awake?"

"Huh? What's up?"

"It's me, Pop. Say, I'm going to get married!"

"Married? The hell you say!" the old man bellowed. "Who to?"

I crept to the door so that I could see into the room. Pop had pried himself up off his pillow and was sitting on the edge of the bed. Slowly, he groped for his battered Stetson.

"I guess you know who to," John chuckled.

"Old Sharpe's daughter, eh?"

"That's right."

"H'm. You got any money?" the old man growled as he jammed his hat onto his head.

"Nope," said John, "as a matter of fact, I don't have any cash at all."

"Well you sure as hell won't get very far without money," Pop snorted.

I heard his feet hit the floor with a thud, and just had time to duck away from the door when he came charging through with John at his heels.

"Sit down girl!" he boomed as he passed me.

Out in the front hall, Pop halted in front of the big safe which stood in one corner. Twirling the dial deftly, he

19

opened its door and took out $300. He passed it over to his son without another word.

"You'll have to sign this consent too, Pop," John said, holding out the paper. "See, Mr. Sharpe has already signed it."

Pop looked at the sheet of paper doubtfully. He was not a man who signed things without a struggle. For a moment my heart stopped beating. Suddenly the old man seized the paper and signed it with the pen that John held ready. Miracle number two had happened right on schedule!

"Where you going to get married?" he asked, and it seemed to me his glance half-included me in the question.

"Medicine Hat," John told him.

"When'll you be back?"

"In a few days."

They looked at each other a moment without speaking, then Pop nodded briefly and turned toward the bedroom.

"See you, Pop," John said, and I added a rather feeble "Goodbye."

"Goodbye," he grunted, and I don't know if I was included in this farewell or not.

Soon we were rattling along toward Medicine Hat with the loose road-gravel beating a steady tattoo on our fenders while the headlights bored into the wall of darkness ahead.

The wedding took place the next day at the home of Aunt Flora and Uncle Harry Minor, in front of their living room fireplace to be exact. I hadn't seen Aunt Flora or Uncle Harry since the branding, and I greeted them happily. My spirits were dampened a little by the announcement that there would be about thirty minutes delay in the wedding because our best man, Murray Minor, had wet his pants.

It wasn't as bad as it sounded though. The tailor had spilled some water on Minor's trousers as he was giving them a final press. Finally, our best man did arrive, breathless and perspiring. And so the ceremony began. My sister, Evelyn, was my bridesmaid. Her husband, Dick Grey, gave me away.

"Dearly beloved... " began the Reverend Taylor of St. John's Presbyterian Church, and a hush fell over the room. I was so excited I only half heard the rest of it.

Then suddenly John was putting the ring onto my finger

20

and everybody started kissing everybody else and making a big fuss.

Generous as usual, Aunt Flora had made most of the wedding preparations herself. Instead of the traditional wedding fruitcake, she had baked a chocolate cake with fluffy white icing, because she knew it was John's favorite.

At the reception, John stood up, blushing and nervous, to reply to the toast to the bride.

"Well, she's a good calf wrestler anyway," was all he said, then sat down abruptly. It must have been a popular speech, though, for everybody clapped and cheered.

When we were getting ready to leave on our honeymoon, one of John's sisters tried to talk him out of making the trip.

"Pop's not a young man anymore," she pointed out. "He shouldn't be left alone on the ranch at such a busy time."

But John would have none of it. "The place will just have to manage without me for two weeks," he told her. "I figure I'll have only one honeymoon in my lifetime, and nothing's going to stop me from enjoying it!"

"Me, too," I said. But with her words came the first little cloud on my horizon. After two weeks there would still be Pop to face up to, and I did not know how I was going to manage it. My legs always turned to jelly whenever he fixed me with his eye.

Then my forebodings were forgotten in the excitement of the coming adventure. We were going to Calgary, and then on to Banff—romantic, faraway places to me! Up until now, my wanderings had been largely confined to the three miles between our farm and the village of Abbey. At long last I was going to see these magic cities which had existed only in the tales of traveling neighbors!

The vehicle of our adventure, of course, was John's 1938 De Soto, black as an Angus steer and just as ornery. His father had given it to him for his fifteenth birthday with a typical, "You keep the hell out of my car an' I'll keep the hell out of yours!"

Decorated with "Just Married" signs, tin cans and other marital paraphernalia, it advertised our newly-found status loud and clear. As we pushed the old thing up hills (there was no Trans Canada Highway in those days), limped into dusty service stations, or sputtered and coughed our way through small towns, people smiled and waved.

"Good Luck!" they shouted.

Then, at last, Calgary lay before us, and beyond it the great sweep of the Rocky Mountains. The awesome size of the city (about 60,000 people, I imagine) overwhelmed us. We went shopping in multi-leveled department stores and ate in posh restaurants. Hand in hand we wandered down the multitude of paved streets, gawking up at the towering buildings. Was there ever a place like it?

John was ingenious at thinking up reasons for taking me on elevator rides. On our second day in Calgary, the elevator operator, ascending with this pair of giggling teenagers for about the umpteenth time since her shift began, finally queried, "Are you two *really* married?"

As we headed westward toward the Rockies, the old De Soto faced the toughest grind of its bumpy career. John never believed in indulging any vehicle, even one in the twilight of its existence. He kept that ol' accelerator flat against the floorboards as we raced around tricky mountain bends, rattled down precipitous hills or labored slowly up steep grades.

Finally, the inevitable happened. The De Soto went on strike and demanded some fringe benefits, such as all the gasoline it could drink—not by way of the gas pump, but poured down the throat of its carburetor from a can.

And that's how we came to Banff, with the right flap of the engine hood open and me pouring soothing draughts of gasoline over the sputtering carburetor. On the down grades, we would roar madly along while I clutched the slippery fender for dear life, my long brown hair streaming in the wind. When the old car picked up speed, John would burst into gleeful song, and the car would reply with an occasional hearty backfire. As for me, I was content just to hang on and pray.

After two blissful weeks we came home to the broad country and the dusty Sandhills. We soon found that the local grapevine had produced a bumper crop of predictions, gossip and innuendo. "They're much too young, just a pair of kids, in fact," one group maintained. "It's puppy love, and it will never work," said another. Many in the district were already predicting the arrival of a new member of our household.

Chapter III:

No Home on the Range

We arrived at the Minor Ranch after midnight so it was next morning before I had to face my new family. John and I lay in bed and listened to the cacophony that told us Pop was ready to meet the demands of another day. The old man never did anything quietly.

First came a hearty whoop and a holler. On the prairies, these words are used to describe a short distance, but Pop's "whoop and holler" could be heard two or three sections away. This was followed by a couple of monotone bars of "My Darling Clementine," vigorously, if not musically delivered. Then Puppy, the collie dog who slept beside his bed, was greeted with true profanity and affection.

"Come on you ol' son-of-a-bitch! Let's go!"

We heard the dog answer and then the sound of their passage through the kitchen below. The dog's prancing feet rattled across the hard linoleum of the floor to the squeaky tune of a chamber pail that Pop always carried out to dump each morning.

Pop cussed everything that stood in his way, sang a few more lusty bars of "My Darling Clementine" and somehow still managed to keep up a rapid-fire conversation with the sleepy dog. Stomping back into the kitchen the old man banged the door so hard it could be felt all through the house, way down there in China too, for all I know. Then we heard him clomp to the foot of the stairs, and his powerful voice boomed:

"Roll out! What kind of an outfit do you think we're running here?" It was five o'clock.

He returned noisily to the kitchen and poked vigorously at the stove before plunging outside again. Soon we heard him over at the bunkhouse yelling at the men.

"Come on you bastards!" he roared, "Roll out! Gonna sleep all day?"

John jumped out of bed at once, threw on his clothes and went down the stairs two at a crack, but I tried to waste as much time as possible. I wanted to put off that dreaded moment when I would have to face them all. A few minutes later I heard Pop's rough, friendly greetings as the men began to stream into the dining room for breakfast.

John was waiting for me below. By the time we entered the room about fifteen people were seated at a table that seemed to me about a mile long. I was used to the small table in our kitchen at home with just Dad and me seated in one corner. This meal seemed more like a banquet, or a church supper, only you don't hear such salty language at a church supper, not even in the Sandhills country.

Way down at the far end of this great table sat Pop, with a fork in one hand and a knife in the other as if he really meant business. His piercing blue eyes were fixed on me.

"Morning!" he boomed.

"Good morning, Mr. Minor," I said in a timid little voice, wishing I could suddenly disappear.

"MISTER Minor!" he chuckled loudly, "Now ain't that something!"

There was a roar of laughter from the hired men who were all ranged along one side of the table. I would have to get to know him a lot better before I could call him Pop like the rest.

As John and I sat down on the family side, I became aware that the men were looking at me curiously, and with no little amusement. Some were smirking and exchanging glances with John. Remembering my first ranch breakfast when I had been offered the "calf fries," I knew I was in for a long session of snickers and stares.

Ranch folks take their breakfasts seriously. There would be howls of protest if they were asked to get by on the two slices of overdone toast, soft-boiled egg and pot of weak coffee that I always prepared for Dad.

Everyone had been busy polishing off half a grapefruit when we arrived. After that, came a big platter heaped with hot baking powder biscuits. This was followed by a steaming bowl of fried onions, a platter of T-bone steaks, juicy and rare, a bowl of fried potatoes, a plate of corn mush, a plate stacked high with buttered toast and a big galvanized pot of thick, black coffee. "Breakfast," thought I. "This is more like a medieval feast!"

But the glory of it was wasted on me. In spite of all this delicious-smelling food, I found my appetite had completely disappeared. I couldn't eat in this huge room, around this great, long table with all these grinning people staring at me. I heaved a big sigh of relief when the meal was finally over.

After breakfast, John and I started to gather our things together. We planned to move to the Old Ranch, five miles away. This was the house that John's mother had come to as a bride in 1912. When the Minor brothers separated on expansion, John's parents had moved to the present ranch headquarters, which had a much bigger house built by Harry Minor.

When Pop realized that John and I were getting ready to leave, he bellowed: "Where the hell are you two going?"

"To the Old Ranch," John said. "That's where we're going to live."

"The hell you say!" the old man exploded. "I thought you were going to live here with me!"

"We figured to try it on our own for awhile," John told him.

"Hmpf!" Pop snorted and stomped off, his disapproval showing in the set of his shoulders. But he did not say another word.

The Old Ranch was old in more ways than one. In fact, it was plumb worn out! John and I drove up to the door in a battered half-ton truck. I had a few misgivings about the house's dilapidated exterior, but Dad had always told us that you should never base a judgment on outside appearances. As we jumped out of the truck we were clowning with each other, joking about crossing the threshold of our first home.

"No kidding," said John, "this is what folks call a solemn occasion."

Suddenly he scooped me up in his arms, shoved the creaking door open with one foot and stepped dramatically through the doorway. With a flourish he kissed the bride, and then set me gently down on a pile of smelly rubbish. As I looked around I became even more solemn than the occasion demanded.

Dad had been right. The mild decay of the exterior gave little hint of the terrible mess which greeted our eyes inside. A mountain of junk covered the stove, table and floor. There were tin cans, broken glass, old boots and shoes, broken chairs, bottles, paper cartons and piles of just plain garbage. No one had lived here for a long time. Every step we took flushed out a family of squealing mice that scuttled away seeking new hiding places under the debris. All the windows in the house had been broken, and a thick coating of sand had drifted in.

Directly in front of us lay the crowning horror of the whole scene, a discarded body cast modeled in the shape of a small, skinny female.

"Hey, that was Mrs. Gardippie!" John laughed. Then he proceeded to tell me of this couple who worked for the Minors many years and lived in this house. Mrs. Gardippie had been a skinny little old lady right enough, but as active as a grasshopper in a ripening oat field. One day she was thrown from her horse and broke her neck. To an active person like Mrs. Gardippie, wearing a cast was a bigger tragedy than the fall itself. One day she could endure the thing no longer, so she ordered her husband to saw it off, which he did.

"They left it lying right there where it fell, and adjusted their lives around it," John finished with a chuckle.

Suddenly, John gave a yell, and charged wildly at the cast. He kicked it up into the air, as mice scattered all over the place, squealing in panic. The body cast spiraled grotesquely across the room and crashed into the wall. It broke under the impact, spraying plaster of Paris dust all over the junk below. Galvanized into action, we set to work. Methodically, we began picking up the debris and hauling it outside.

By the day's end we had tossed out enough junk to fill a couple of trunks. Our final task was to set up an old bed in one of the rooms. Then we fell onto it exhausted, too tired to bother about the long, wispy cobwebs which hung from the ceiling, the broken windows or the squeaking mice that bustled about.

The next thing I remember was the sound of a voice pounding steadily around the rim of my consciousness. It had a hollow sound and seemed to be mixed up with a vision of Mrs. Gardippie's body cast dancing across the room. My mind cleared suddenly and I heard the voice again. This time I recognized it.

"You people gonna sleep all day?" it boomed.

"That's Pop!" John cried, springing out of bed.

"What time is it?" I muttered sleepily.

John peered at his watch. "My gosh! It's six o'clock!" he exclaimed. "I'd better get moving!"

When I came out of the bedroom a few moments later, the old man was briskly prodding the fire he had set in the sagging, rusty kitchen range.

"I just dropped by to see if you were all settled," he said. "Thought I might have a spot of breakfast too. Lucky I decided to come over or you might have slept in."

I looked at him sleepily, trying to remember something, but John beat me to it.

"Hell, Pop, we didn't bring any groceries!" he said.

His father nodded, "I figured you wouldn't. Come on and give me a hand!"

They tramped out of the kitchen, while I sat there still trying to collect my wits. In a moment they returned, each carrying a hundred-pound sack of flour. "Anyway," I thought wryly, "it looks as if Pop expects our marriage to last."

"You might as well help too," John told me. "Pop never does things by halves!"

"There's enough stuff here to feed an army!" I protested when I caught sight of all the food piled in the back of the pick-up.

"Army hell!" Pop snorted. "I'm only sending out a hay crew of four men. That'll sort of give you a chance to get your feet on the ground before the main bunch arrive!"

All at once I felt a little weak at the knees and wanted to sit down. He even expects me to bake bread for them I thought wildly, and I've never baked a loaf in my whole life! The very idea of trying to bake on that old cook stove just about made me sick.

"Where'll we put the men?" John asked his father.

"In the old bunk shack behind the house. Maybe that girl will have time to give it a few licks before they arrive."

By this time, "that girl" was headed for the house before any more horrible details were revealed. But not before I heard Pop tell John that he had a lot of ranch work lined up, that John couldn't spend any more time helping me with the house. Now I knew what people meant when they talked about the "honeymoon being over."

After the stove had cooled down from breakfast, I set to work trying to chip the rust off it. At least I didn't have to remove any roast mouse from the oven. Pop had chased a family of rodents out before he lit the fire.

The old man appeared in the doorway as I was still peering gingerly into the oven.

"John's mother baked her first loaves on that," he boomed. "I just dropped in to tell you we're sending over a couple of pigs, some chickens and a team of work horses from the other place. You'll find them handy things to have around." And he left.

"Oh my gosh," I thought wearily, "what next?"

All morning I labored trying to bring forth my first cake. Just when I thought I had succeeded, ashes would fall through the worn grates onto the top of it. It was impossible to keep an even heat in that pesky oven. When I finally gave up, I had a cake with a burned top and a bottom of ash grey dough. The roast beef I had cooked for dinner also came out covered with ashes. All I needed was a sackcloth dress to make the sacrifice complete.

Because it was wartime, fall of 1944, there was no hope of our buying anything new for the house. We had to make do with what we had, and that was precious little. Most of the so-called kitchen equipment was stuff John's mother had used as a bride. There were a couple of rusty iron frying pans, some beat-up pots and pans, a galvanized washboard and an assortment of heavy flat irons that had to be heated on top of the stove. Hardly enough to win me any awards as Homemaker of the Month.

My lack of equipment was complemented by a woeful lack of experience. In those first days of cooking for the haying crew my failures were many and my triumphs few. No matter how hard I tried, my bread never came out high and golden-hued like the pictures in my cookbook. It always emerged from the oven black on top with a somber coating of ashes. Generally, the bread ended up being kicked around the yard as a football. Maybe I'd never make it as a cook, but I began to feel I might have a fine future as a manufacturer of sporting goods.

No matter what happened, John never ridiculed my efforts, not even when he tried to put a knife into one of my first baking powder biscuits and the thing went flying across the room. And, in spite of the fact his father had said he would not have time to help me, he spent almost every evening painting and cleaning with me. When we could do no more we would fall exhausted into bed. A few short hours of sleep and John was completely restored. At the stroke of five a.m. he would spring lightly out of bed, exclaiming what a beautiful day it was. While I lay groggily thinking about my coming fight with the old stove, about the heat and cobwebs and dust, he would be out whistling in the kitchen as he got breakfast going.

As most of our supplies came from the main ranch, we had to make many trips over there. Usually, John would drive me in the old De Soto, but something told me it was only a matter of time until I would be expected to make the trip alone. And I knew even less about cars than I did about cooking or bulldogging calves.

It happened about two weeks after we had returned from our honeymoon. When the car was all loaded up, John decided he would stay at the ranch and give them a hand for a few hours. He motioned for me to get behind the wheel, and then he explained the gear-shift positions. Now that the dreaded moment had actually arrived, I was terrified. Everything he said went in one ear and out the other.

Finally, when he figured I had had enough instruction, John swung his arms toward the west and shouted, "She's all yours! Take her home!"

For a minute or two I just sat there petrified. I had never even tried to drive a car! Although Dad had owned a Model "A," he would never have dreamed of letting any of his daughters touch it. He himself never drove it over thirty miles an hour, cautiously steering down the road with both hands grimly clutching the wheel. If he had gotten even the tiniest mark on the car, the event would have been hailed as a disaster.

That's one big difference between ranchers and farmers. Ranchers are a go-for-broke, hell-for-leather bunch who tackle problems the same way a bull tackles a corral fence. Farmers tend to do a heap of careful thinking before they make a move, and I was a farmer's daughter. The trouble was I was too terrified to do any kind of thinking, so I just did as I was told.

Reaching down with a shaky hand, I released the brake. We shot forward in a cloud of dust. I didn't even know the old car had a throttle, let alone that this throttle was pulled way out!

The speedometer was soon registering fifty miles per hour, even though I hadn't touched a foot to the accelerator. The narrow, deeply-rutted road began to unreel before me like the track of a roller coaster. Every time we came to a sharp bend the car would veer off into the sagebrush. Only by yanking on the wheel as hard as I could was I able to get the old vehicle back into the safety of the ruts. Sometimes when we veered off the road, it would swing suddenly to meet us again, and the car would hit the ruts at a crazy angle, jolting me up out of the seat so that I banged my head against the roof.

The roller coaster effect was sharpened by the steepness of the hills and the depth of the hollows. One moment I was peering through the spokes of the steering wheel into the blue, blue sky, not knowing what would be in front of the car when it dipped back down the other side of the hill. The next moment I was staring into the ground.

I couldn't find a way to slow the car. Although I pumped the brakes desperately, the stubborn vehicle still raced along like a bronc with the bit between its teeth. I began to wonder how I was going to stop the thing when, and if, we reached home. Would I have to run into the fence? By this time, something was noisily dragging along below. I didn't know if it had hooked onto the branch of a tree or if the old De Soto was gradually falling apart. And I didn't really care as long as this wild gallop across the Sandhills would stop.

Suddenly, I spotted one of our hired men crossing a clearing ahead of me with a load of feed. I jammed both feet on the brakes as hard as I could, stretching my body out like a poker and bracing my shoulders tightly against the back of the seat. The engine roared in protest, but the old car slowed to an anguished crawl.

"There's something the matter with this car!" I shouted, desperately. " I don't put my foot anywhere near the accelerator, but it keeps going faster and faster!"

The man jumped off his wagon and came running over. Reaching through the window, he pushed in a little black knob on the dash. The engine's howl dwindled to a purr, and I was able to bring the car to a stop with ease.

"That there is the throttle, ma'am," he said, looking at me queerly. "You're taking a big chance driving with it pulled away out like that!"

Later that day, John looked the car over to see if he could locate the source of the banging noise I had heard coming from underneath.

"Is there much damage?" I asked anxiously.

"Well," he said, "the muffler is torn off for one thing, and there's a broken springleaf. But hell," he added with a grin, "You don't really need these things to run the car."

On my next trip for supplies I wasn't as lucky. Though I had been instructed in the mysteries of the throttle, I had still not mastered the "feel" of the gas pedal. Until I approached some stationary object, I had no way of judging the car's speed. Such an object stood at the entrance to our yard in the form of a massive steel gate. As I bore down on it, I suddenly realized I was going too fast, and pumped the brakes desperately. The crash jarred me all the way back to my wisdom teeth. This time the car suffered a smashed headlight, a crumpled fender and a punctured radiator. Water gushed from the open wound.

I expected John to blow his top, but he didn't say very much. He just started making plans to tow the De Soto into Abbey for repairs.

"This time it's a bit more serious," he told me. "A car doesn't really need fenders, and you can make out with only one headlight, but you sure as hell can't get very far with a busted radiator. I'll get one of the trucks and tow 'er into town. All you have to do is sit behind the wheel and steer."

"But shouldn't you get a more experienced driver?" I protested. "I don't want to drive anymore!" I said, almost in tears.

"Nope. All the men are busy at their jobs. Anyhow, the only way to become experienced is to do it."

John hitched the car to an old army truck that we used for everything and we headed for town. I sat stony-faced and silent behind the De Soto's wheel, furious at having been roped into a job I knew I was not equipped to handle, but John paid no attention.

A few miles along the road a pup darted out suddenly in front of the truck. John slammed on his brakes without even thinking of his dutiful little wife dragging along behind. The pup was saved, but the old De Soto gave up the second headlight and had fresh scars added to its already mottled complexion.

By now I was in a state of mild shock, and kept repeating, "I didn't know you were going to stop . . . I didn't know you were going to stop . . . "

I began to think I was the most incompetent person in the world.

"It wasn't your fault," John assured me cheerfully. "Next time I stop I'll give you plenty of warning."

"Next time" came sooner then expected. As we rounded a bend, John spotted two women trudging along the road to town. Right away he started signaling to me that he was going to stop and pick them up. As I was so worried about keeping the car on the curving road I didn't see him. This time, the truck and the car embraced each other with real vigor. The whole front end of the De Soto jetted skyward, completely blocking my view ahead. Just as well, I thought grimly. I knew John carried a varmint gun in the truck, and right now I figured I qualified as a varmint. I couldn't blame *this* crash on a pulled throttle, failing brakes, or John not signaling.

But John took the disaster calmly. Maybe his smile was a little tight at the corners as he helped the two women up into the cab of the truck. As we limped down the main street of Abbey, everybody came out to have a look at us.

"Must have had a head-on with a train," I heard one oldtimer say.

The De Soto's hood was up, its grill and headlights were smashed, the fenders were crumpled and water still dripped from below, but most damaged of all was my pride!

Chapter IV:

Git Along Little Dogie

I may have been tough on cars, but it was not intentional on my part. One of the hardest things for me to accept was the way Pop Minor deliberately abused *his* car. Maybe he secretly resented the intrusion of this noisy iron cayuse on his beloved range. My father had trained me to guard any material possessions as if they were the Crown jewels. And a car, being very expensive, was pampered all the time. It was used only on special occasions, and when fall arrived it was put up on blocks to shield it from the rigors of winter.

But Pop Minor figured if you bought something you should use it. To him, having a car sitting around just for pleasure driving was a sheer waste of money. He put his to work—with a vengeance. Most of the time it substituted for a saddle horse. Pop seldom rode a horse after I knew him. He had a rupture which made riding too painful, so he drove his car where he would ordinarily have ridden a horse. Being unable to ride angered him, so I think he liked to humiliate the helpless vehicle whenever he could. When you got into it, you might find windmill parts, tools, calf skins, a sack of potatoes, oil and water cans or anything else he wanted to carry.

One day we all piled into Pop's Ford to have a look at some cattle out on the range. By "all" I mean the immediate family—Pop, John and myself, and of course, Pop's dog, Puppy. It was no joy ride. I sat silently between the two men while they discussed ranch business across me at the top of their lungs. Puppy stood in the rear with his paws up on the back of our seat, panting and drooling down my neck. John was driving.

35

As we bounced along the rough trails of the sandhills, the chrome rim on the inside of the steering wheel, which was cracked, began to rattle. The rattle annoyed Pop. In the middle of a sentence about moving cattle, he leaned over abruptly and roared at John:

"Tear that there son-of-a-bitch off!"

Without interrupting the flow of conversation, John calmly ripped the piece off the steering wheel and tossed it out the open window. By now I was sure that I was sitting between a couple of lunatics. If I had had a mother to run home to, this would have been the time to do it.

Suddenly we topped a rise and found ourselves in the center of a herd of galloping antelope.

"Get 'em!" yelled Pop, and John pressed the accelerator right to the floor boards.

We plunged off the road in a cloud of dust, bumping across the rough prairie sod until I thought my teeth would jar loose. Pop and John were laughing and yelling with the joy of the chase. They liked to test the speed of these sleek wild creatures. The dog was bouncing all over the place, barking excitedly. All at once we crashed down into a bull hole and came to a jarring stop, which sent the four of us flying around in the car. When we had settled back into our seats with the dust, Pop said disgustedly:

"This goddamn car ain't got no shocks at all! They sure don't make 'em like they used to!"

Once I had been initiated into the use of a car, John thought it was time I learned to ride a horse. He wanted to have me with him as much as possible, so he encouraged me to get my house work done up quickly so that I could go out on the range with him. Although I loved to be with John, I felt so green about everything that I inwardly quailed at the prospect. But I didn't want him to think he had married a tenderfoot who was afraid to try anything, so we went riding every day. I soon learned it's not your feet that get tender when you spend a few hours in the saddle.

That old cliché about being "born in the saddle" comes about as close as anything to describing John's riding skill. He could never understand how anybody could get tired riding a horse, or be nervous of the animal. We would go out riding for two or three hours at a stretch, and John loved every minute of it. In contrast, I was always afraid of my mount bucking me off—or worse still, taking off across the country at a mad gallop with me clinging desperately to the saddle horn like the tender heroine in a Western movie.

If we could have just gone for a peaceful ride around the ranch to look things over I think I would have made more rapid progress in the saddle. As it was, John always managed to find some work to do. It might be a yearling that needed castrating, a cow with a bone stuck in her throat, or one with a big gash that needed sewing up. That is what ranchers ride through their herds for, but I didn't know it then.

John always attended to the trouble right there on the spot, and I had to help him. Most of the time he was riding a "green" horse, that is, a horse-in-training that knew as much about herding cattle as I did. Such animals were only half-disciplined and I was terrified of them. John would rope the cow that needed to be treated and would tell me to get up on his horse and keep the rope taut while he performed the operation.

"I don't want to get up there," I would protest. "That horse is dangerous."

"Go on, get up there," he would say impatiently, "He won't bother you. Just show him who's boss!"

Gingerly, I would climb up into the saddle, shaking with fright and I would stay in that condition all the time John worked on the critter he was treating. Sometimes when he released the patient, the ungrateful animal showed fight and would take after John or my horse with a bellow of rage. If the cow came towards us, the jittery horse would jump out of the way, sometimes spilling its more jittery rider. Then the cow would take after me. It seems I was always running for my life that summer.

By the time we had performed several of these ranch "chores," my seat would be sore and my legs rubbed raw. I would be so exhausted I couldn't even pretend I was making out all right and tears would well up into my eyes. I would tell myself that I didn't care if I *never* proved myself. That, of course, was what I had been trying to do ever since John and I got married—prove that I could make a good ranch wife.

37

So each morning found me riding again. As soon as he had eaten breakfast, John would rush out to saddle our horses while I limped around tidying the house. There seemed to be no limit to his energy.

"All set!" he'd shout as soon as the horses were ready.

"Be there in a minute!" I would sing out cheerfully, while making faces to myself as I slipped into my riding boots.

One day I decided I would prove to John how much I had learned about ranching. I wanted to do a ranch job completely on my own with no help from anyone. John planned to ride to a nearby range so he could check a lame cow, and I had decided to stay home and bake a chocolate cake. Suddenly, I thought it would be a good idea if we reversed our roles.

"Tell you what," I said stoutly. "Why don't you try your hand at baking the cake, and I'll saddle my horse and ride out to check that cow!"

"Great idea!" he nodded. "I always figured baking was a lot easier than you girls let on."

Before I had a chance to change my mind, he was bustling around the kitchen, and I was on my way out to the corral to saddle my first horse. Although I had watched John saddle up lots of times, I had never actually gotten around to doing it myself. But it looked simple enough. And I was determined I would slap on that saddle without showing a sign of hesitation because I had an idea John was looking out the window and grinning.

Taking the saddle from the rail, I swung it at the horse, trying to act as if I had done this a hundred times before. The saddle was a bit heavier than I figured so it sort of took me along with it. We hit the poor animal somewhere near the top of the rib cage and he jumped back with a snort.

"Easy there, fella," I quavered, not daring to look toward the house.

On my next try, the saddle landed squarely on the horse's back. How tight to make the cinch was my next problem, but I just pulled on it until the skin on the animal's belly began to wrinkle a little. I didn't want to give the poor critter a stomach ache. Then I mounted up and rode out of the yard like a veteran.

Before we had gone very far the horse decided to call my bluff. He took off across the prairie at a full gallop, and I found myself smack in the middle of the Grade B movie scene I had dreaded all along—with no handsome hero to rescue me. There was nothing I could do to control him so I just hung on for dear life, hoping he would soon run himself out.

As we thundered up over hills and down through brush-filled hollows I became painfully aware that my cinch-tightening left much to be desired.

Gradually, the saddle began to slip sideways. If anything, that pesky horse increased his pace. For a moment or two I rode halfway down the animal's flank, like a Comanche attacking a wagon train. Then I let go of the saddle horn and tumbled to the ground. While I lay on the grass collecting my wits, I gingerly felt all over my body to see if I had any broken bones. When there appeared to be none, I rose slowly and looked around for my horse.

The mutinous critter had stopped only a few paces from me and was innocently nibbling at the grass. His saddle was hanging upside down under his belly, and it creaked and swayed as he moved. As I approached warily, he fixed me with one bloodshot eye. When he figured I had come too close, he tried to back away, but the swinging saddle impeded his progress so that I was able to grab the trailing reins. Not wanting to entrust myself to his loving care anymore, I meekly led him home.

John had been watching for me at the window. As I came limping into the yard with the horse walking smugly behind, he came quietly out and took the reins. I looked at him quickly to see if I could detect any signs of amusement, but he was as grave as an Indian at a treaty signing.

"You okay?" he asked, as he unsaddled the horse.

"I think I'll survive," I told him.

"Good," he grinned suddenly, "come on inside and I'll treat you to a piece of chocolate cake."

"Don't tell me he made a success of that, too," I groaned to myself. I felt a bit better when I saw that his culinary effort showed definite signs of sagging in the middle, and the top was much too black, even for a chocolate cake.

"By the way," he said casually, "how was that cow?"

"What cow?"

"The lame one you went out to check."

"Oh my gosh, I forgot all about her. In fact, I never even got there."

"No matter," he shrugged. "I expect she'll survive, too."

At that moment he bit into a piece of burnt cake and made a wry face. "Tell you what," he added, "from now on I'll do the riding and you can bake the cakes."

"Agreed," I nodded eagerly, and we both laughed.

"There's just one thing that bothers me," I said.

"What's that?"

"How tight do you make a saddle cinch?"

"Just as tight as you can damn well pull it!" he told me.

"Guess I'll never make a rider," I sighed.

But it was not very long until I was out again, insisting this ranching business was not so complicated that a really determined person (meaning myself) couldn't learn all about it. I wanted to prove to John that I could do my share around the place. One afternoon, John and the men were going to move cattle from Mason Valley to Home Valley, a distance of about five miles. I told John it might be a good idea if I went along because you never knew when an extra rider might be needed.

"Yep," he nodded with a twinkle, "an extra hand can save the day sometimes."

All right, I thought to myself, noting the twinkle, I'll show the whole bunch of you. This time you will have to admit I've made progress. John let me get my horse out and throw the saddle onto him, but he insisted on tightening the cinch. Then we rode off into the hills.

Brought up as I was on three-quarters of a section of flat farmland I could never figure out how anyone could find his way in the Great Sandhills. At that time, the Minor Ranch spread out over 50,000 acres of slopes, valleys, bushes, trees and twisting trails, and they all looked the same. I generally got lost as soon as I got outside the gate.

The trouble with this roundup was that everyone seemed to know what was going on except me. John had told the men where we were supposed to be taking the herd, but his brief explanation to me meant very little because I knew nothing about working cattle. Even the critters themselves seemed to know what was expected of them. As they watched the riders spread out behind, one or two started to move in the desired direction. Soon the whole herd followed.

I decided the safest thing to do was to get behind them, and just ride along. After all, I knew I was only bluffing about being able to herd cattle. The trick was to keep the others from knowing. This worked fine for awhile. Then suddenly I began to realize it was getting dark—that I could no longer see the other riders, and of course, they could no longer see me.

My big bluff might have worked if something hadn't scared my horse just as we topped the last ridge and were heading down into Home Valley. Maybe it was a rattler late getting home, or a badger lifting his head from his burrow. Maybe the horse just pretended to be scared. I don't think he liked me very much, when I come to think of it. Anyway, I soon found myself in my normal riding position—flat on the ground—as my mount bolted off into the night. The cattle and other riders had moved on, too, leaving me alone in the eerie darkness.

The first thing I became aware of was a stabbing pain in my arm. I was sure the arm was broken this time, but when I struggled to an upright position that painful member came right along with me without dangling grotesquely, so I concluded it was only bruised after all. Next, I began to feel my aloneness, and a chill ran through me. I imagined that all kinds of wild animals were creeping down from the hills to attack me. How would the others be able to find me out here in all this vast night?

Then I imagined what would happen if they *did* find me. I would have to admit I was quite hopeless as a rancher's wife and that I couldn't even look after myself. Was it even worthwhile getting rescued? For over an hour I wandered aimlessly through the darkness, holding my injured arm tenderly and sobbing. I was a great sobber in those days. If I had been going full blast in the thirties there would probably never have been a drought.

After awhile I saw lights winding through the valley below. I counted three vehicles, and as they spread out across the valley floor I knew they were looking for me. How badly I wanted to be found! I didn't care what anybody thought of me or of my riding ability now. All my pride had been cried out, and I just wanted to get home to my warm bed. I shouted and headed down toward them.

Soon one of the cars caught my silhouette in its bouncing headlights. It ground to a stop and John jumped out and ran frantically toward me. Then he was holding me, and telling me how afraid he had been that I was lying out on the grass somewhere badly hurt. He picked me up and carried me to the waiting car. I was so relieved I began to sob once more. He put his arm around me as we drove home. It felt so good I wondered if it might be a good idea for me to hit the saddle first thing next morning, but it was several days before John asked me to go riding again.

Chapter V:

That Goddam Girl

And that is how *my* long, hot summer went—with me feeling the weight of Pop Minor's constant judgment as I struggled to learn everything a rancher's wife was supposed to know. I kept hoping that just once the old man would give me a few words of encouragement. But he never did.

One day, John's sister told me, laughingly, that Pop had referred to me as "that goddam girl." Shocked beyond belief, I ran to John and told him how I had been humiliated.

"I can't stay around that cussing old man another minute!" I sobbed.

John burst out laughing.

"Don't let that worry you, honey," he said, "He doesn't mean a thing by it. The more he cusses people, the better he likes 'em."

I didn't believe John, but I stayed anyway—telling myself I must be a real glutton for punishment.

Pop had a habit of coming to our place early in the morning to pick up John. On Sundays he appeared to arrive much earlier than usual. Just when we thought we might have one morning to sleep in, we would waken to the sound of Pop's vehicle coming up into our yard. As if it were a sin to be caught in bed at daybreak, we would leap out of bed guiltily and struggle into our clothes.

"Nobody up yet around this outfit?" his voice would boom. "Home Valley windmill's broke down."

At such an hour on a Sunday morning I loathed the sight of him even more than usual. Inside, I would be seething with anger at him for disturbing our well-earned rest, but I bottled it all up.

Out to the kitchen I would trot without saying a word. I knew how John loved his father, and I did not want either of them to know how I really felt.

Pop sure didn't try to make himself more popular with me. He would often turn up at our door about fifteen minutes before mealtime with a whole crowd of visitors behind him and yell, "Can we get anything to eat around this goddam house?"

It did not matter that I might be scrubbing clothes or painting, or that I had prepared just enough food for the crew. To Pop such things were mere details. The sight of all these unexpected guests, and the last-minute confusion which followed, always sent me into a tailspin for the rest of the afternoon.

But I would put on a smiling, hospitable front, secretly cursing the day Pop Minor was born. What I should have done, of course, was loudly cuss the old man up one side of the room and down the other. Except that he would have loved it, I found out later.

By the end of the summer I was physically and mentally exhausted from trying to adjust to this totally different environment. I had had to learn so many things, and get along with such large crowds of people. But most of my trouble came from being constantly nervous and angry whenever Pop was around.

Finally the hay crew put the last forkful of sweet-scented hay on the last haystack in Home Valley. I gave a big sigh of relief, for this meant they would all move back to the main ranch. At last John and I were alone in our home!

One day in October, John told me they were going to be dehorning some yearlings in the corrals at the main ranch. As I had never watched this procedure, I drove out there, eager to learn all I could of the cattle business. Jumping excitedly out of the car, I climbed to the top of the corral fence. The men already had an animal at the end of the chute, his head held tightly in the squeeze. This is a device which holds cattle still while you subject them to all sorts of indignities, such as innoculation, insemination, ear tattooing, branding, and dehorning when they are too big to wrestle to the ground.

Just as I sat down, I heard a grinding crunch as John

squeezed the long-handled dehorners around the base of the horn. The critter bellowed loudly with pain. As the horn fell to the ground, blood rushed down the animal's white face, squirting all over John who was busy clamping the dehorners around the other horn. The animal struggled madly, trying to back away from his tormentor. That brief look was all I could take. Feeling suddenly faint, I ran for my car, certain that I never wanted to watch another dehorning.

Later on in the fall, we had to trail three hundred head of four-year-old steers sixteen miles to the railway loading chutes at Abbey. When John said I could help, I was very excited. I had never been on a real trail ride, and was happy that the men thought I would be of some use to them. Then doubts began to assail me.

"What did Pop have to say about me going along?" I asked.

"He said sure, bring her along."

"Bring who along?"

"Why you, of course. What are you getting at?"

"Are you sure he didn't refer to me as "that you-know-what-girl" again?"

"I wasn't listening that close," John said evasively, but I could see he was struggling to suppress a grin.

"No matter," I said grimly, "I'm going anyway."

We were up soon after two a.m. As I charged around preparing breakfast, my stomach was sick with excitement. We left home at daybreak and headed into the dawn. There is a special thrill to mounting a horse in that peaceful stillness just before sunup and looking forward to being a part of all that action—especially for a tenderfoot.

The dawn stillness was soon shattered by the anxious bellowing of the cattle, as if they sensed that this was their last journey. Mingled with their protests were the hoarse shouts of the men and the jingle of saddle gear. We moved the critters slowly, stopping often to let them water.

There are two schools of thought about driving cattle. Some say you should drive them slowly, while others maintain you should get them there and settled as fast as possible. At Tombstone, Arizona, in 1882, two hot-tempered ranchers drew guns over this question and one of them died, which proves that cattlemen can get pretty emotional about their business.

By noon, our point riders—the ones who ride at the head of the herd—had reached the edge of town. As usual, I rode at the rear, or "drag," as it is called in cowboy parlance. This is where most of the dust collects, so I wasn't exactly ready for a beauty contest when we arrived.

Crowds of spectators were waiting outside town to watch the Minors bring in their beef. Pop was in his element. He cussed loudly at the animals, boomed out rough commands and directed the whole show in his usual noisy, but business-like manner. I sat proudly on my horse, feeling a little nervous and shy in front of the crowds who lined our path through the center of town. Of course Pop had no stagefright at all. He loved every moment of it.

When the cattle were all safely delivered to the yards, Pop led us over to the Abbey Cafe for the traditional Minor celebration. As we poured into the cafe, he let out a whoop and a holler. With all eyes trained on him, he bellowed to the smiling waitress, "Bring us all a great big T-bone steak!"

When John was driving any vehicle, Pop never allowed him to poke along at a reasonable pace. If a car came up behind us on the highway, the old man would shout, "Don't let that son-of-a-bitch pass us!" instead of cautioning his son to take it easy, as most fathers would. Or, if there was a vehicle on the road ahead, he would holler, "Pass that son-of-a-bitch!" no matter what speed we were already traveling. With this training behind him, John always drove as fast as possible, regardless of what kind of road he was driving on, or what he was hauling.

A few days before Christmas that first year, John was coming through the snowclad hills in a truck, bouncing crazily along in his usual manner, in spite of the fact he was hauling my Christmas present—a crated piano. As he rounded a sharp bend at top speed, the centrifugal force sent my piano flying out the rear of the truck. It landed in some bushes about twenty feet from the road. John saw it go in his rear view mirror, so he stopped the truck and backed up. Seeing the piano sitting upright away out there in the snow with the crate flattened perfectly on all four sides, he laughed to himself. Then he headed home to get something to pick it up with.

"Quick!" he cried, as he rushed into the house. "We need your help! There's a sick cow out there on the trail!"

He was hopping around as if he expected the cow to die any minute, so I grabbed my coat and rushed out the door behind him. I did wonder a little why he had come to me. I was not noted for being particularly useful in such situations, but my suspicions fled in the excitement of the rescue.

Outside, a couple of the men had just finished hitching a prancing team to a stoneboat—a kind of rough sled used for hauling manure and other bulky objects. John leaped up onto the stoneboat and I followed joyfully. Then we were off in a cloud of fine powdered snow.

When we got to the "sick cow," I was a little shocked to see my Christmas present sitting out unprotected from the elements. A close inspection, however, showed that there wasn't even a scratch on it. And then, the sight of a piano sitting upright in the winter vastness of the Great Sand Hills was so ridiculous we all burst out laughing. In the fun, I even forgot to give John the usual lecture about reckless driving. To complete the scene, I waded through a snowdrift to the piano and stood knee-deep before the keyboard to play a popular Christmas carol, "Joy to the World." I also wanted to see if the thing still worked—after all, I was *my* father's daughter.

With the chill winds of January upon us, John was busy from morning until night, feeding the cattle and keeping the ice off the water tanks at the windmill sites on our winter range. Feed had to be hauled to the cattle by teams of horses pulling sled-mounted hay racks. Uprighting and re-loading racks that had slipped off a slippery grade was all a part of the day's work. At home, our life settled into a relaxed routine. We had put away the last paint can and swept the last cobweb from the corners. The remains of Mrs. Gardippie's body cast had been given a decent burial. Even Pop seemed to mellow a little as we recuperated from our summer labors.

Then a carpenter moved in with us to renovate the house, and we were up to our loving ears in another mess. A bachelor of about fifty, this man had worked for the Minors for many years and was well-respected for his craftsmanship, if not for his manners. He had rigid ways of thinking and acting which he would not compromise for anyone—

not even for Pop Minor.

Because he had been a part of the Minor Ranch for a lot longer than I had, the carpenter expected me to adjust my life to suit him. Now I had two ornery males to contend with, and I hadn't even learned how to cope with the first one.

When he came to breakfast that first morning, John asked him what kind of sleep he'd had. He looked at the both of us with his big eyes brimful of self pity.

"Not very good," he said mournfully. "The mice ran over me in herds of forty or fifty."

He was with us until spring, and never was spring more welcome! All the time he was there he had two workbenches set up: one in the bunkhouse, and another much longer one, which he seldom used, in the middle of my kitchen floor. Most of my time was spent sweeping up the sawdust he trailed from one end of the house to the other. Although I boiled inside, I never dared say anything to this delightful house guest because I knew that Pop respected him for the quality of his work (and probably for his cussedness, too). Most of the time I tried to stay out of our visitor's way to avoid his wrath, and his constant—and boring—lectures on the benefits of the Communist system.

In fact, the mealtime conversation that winter consisted of a continuing discourse on the opportunity-packed life which awaited anyone fortunate enough to live in Russia. This had always been the man's theme, and Pop was used to hearing it. But one day, when the carpenter was a bit more vehement than usual, it really got under Pop's skin.

"Why you ornery old son-of-a-bitch!" he bellowed, "I'll tell you what I'll do. I'll buy you a ticket to Russia—but just one way, understand. You've got to damn well stay there if you go!"

For once I was on Pop's side. It did not rid us of my un-welcome visitor, but we were spared the usual lecture for that one meal.

At bedtime, the carpenter always put his teeth to soak in a tin cup which he placed on the reservoir of the stove near his bed, and one night the cup got accidentally pushed to the back of the stove. When the morning fires were lit, the water in the cup started boiling merrily. Soon the teeth were warped so badly their owner could not get them back into his mouth. He sat down to his T-bone steak breakfast that morning with his lips and cheeks all caved in, and his eyes full of malice—sure that somebody had done it on purpose.

"You'll have to grind that meat for me," he said, in a garbled but demanding voice. And from then on, I grudgingly ground his meat at every meal.

One day, I was sorting through some dishes while he was out of the kitchen. A lot of our extra dishes had been stored in boxes, and I was trying to get what I needed before the old boy returned and told me I was in his way. Then I had to leave the kitchen for a moment, so I put the box of dishes up on his workbench, which he seldom used. While I was gone I heard him open the outside door and step into the kitchen. Suddenly I heard a loud crash and the tinkling of broken china. I rushed back to find that he'd picked up the box and thrown it on the floor, smashing every dish.

That did it as far as I was concerned. Right then and there I decided I would never grind up any more of his meat. Teeth or no teeth, this character was going to have to go it alone. When the next mealtime rolled around I plunked a whole steak down in front of him and walked calmly away. He looked at me in consternation. The last thing this socialist expected was a peasant revolt!

Grinning at my victory, John set up the meat grinder on the edge of the table beside him. For the rest of the winter, our carpenter friend sat stony-faced, methodically grinding his meat as he lectured us about the joys of living in Russia.

"Well," I told myself, "one enemy down and one to go." That you-know-what girl had finally had enough, but my showdown with Pop was a long time in coming. Ranching is closely allied to nature, and natural happenings seem to have their own way of changing things.

Chapter VI:

Nature Takes Its Course

Calves are the "dividends" of the ranching business, and they start to arrive at the first hint of spring. One day we would awake to find that the air had a softer quality—the wind had lost its bite. All at once everybody would begin to talk about calving, and they spoke of it as naturally as they talked about any other ranch job. At first it was a little surprising to me to hear both men and women discussing calving. In the Victorian atmosphere of my own home, no one ever mentioned anything about procreation.

As a child, I knew nothing about the relationship between bulls and cows. To me, bulls were merely dangerous animals which ran in a neighbor's fields, and I had been warned to stay away from them. One morning we would wake up to find a new little calf standing beside one of our milk cows, but I did not question where it came from. If a cow wanted to be bred, it was up to her to crawl through our neighbor's fence at the right time. Nobody would ever dream of opening the gate for her. That would be contributing to bovine delinquency.

I can remember how enraged my father would be if one of his neighbor's bulls got over into our field. And I would not have dared ask him when this magical appearance of spring calves was going to occur. He would have pretended that he didn't hear me, or told me not to talk about such things. But somehow our cows always seemed to produce calves each spring, and to supply us with the fresh milk and cream that Dad expected on the table.

One memorable spring, a cow of ours was not able to have her calf unassisted. After she had struggled for a few days Dad noticed her and called the vet. I was not sure what the problem was, but by sneaking around to the barn where Dad and the vet were talking in hushed voices, I learned that calves really did come out of cows. I can remember feeling guilty and abnormal about my curiosity. All that night I lay awake, listening with wide ears to the comings and goings of Dad and the vet between our kitchen and the barn. What I heard that night was the extent of my formal sex education.

Ranchers, I soon learned, cannot afford to rely on such a hit-and-miss system to get calves. They are much more interested in producing calves than milk and are prepared to go to some pretty gruesome lengths to aid the calving process. Later, I learned a good deal more when the Minor Ranch pioneered an even more unmentionable process called "artificial insemination," which goes a few giant steps beyond introducing a bull into a cow pasture.

My first trip through the Minor calving fields with John was a delightful experience. What a beautiful sight it was to see the newly-born calves running beside their mothers! They would kick their heels up into the air, their snowwhite faces glistening in the warming sun! How exciting it was to see hundreds of these calves after living on a farm where the calf crop never exceeded three per year!

My next trip through was a different kind of experience. As we came up to a heifer lying by herself in the bush, I asked John why she was not out in the field with the rest.

"When a cow is ready to calve, she likes to find a place away from the others," he explained. "I see this one's been having trouble. I'll bet you she's been struggling most of the night."

I thought she didn't look any worse than any expectant mother, but John was out of the truck in a flash. Sitting on the heifer's neck so she couldn't rise, he yelled at me to bring his rope out of the back of the truck. When I ran over with it, he told me to sit on the heifer as he had been doing and not to let her up.

"I don't think she'll give you any trouble," he said, "She's pretty weak."

"Any critter can give me trouble," I told him, but I did as he asked. I sat as heavily as possible for my hundred pounds, but I felt like a mosquito. Then I looked down, and to my amazement, saw a couple of tiny hooves protruding from the heifer's rear.

"John! It's happening!" I cried.

"She's been like that for a long time," he said. "You sit tight!"

Slipping his rope around the little hooves, John started to pull. But the big calf had no intention of coming. Under me, the heifer heaved with the contractions and expansions. I felt sick. Every time she groaned I could almost feel the pain myself.

"Come here and help me," John said, after another unsuccessful pull. "These first-timers always have a tough time calving."

Then we both pulled, and the calf finally slithered out onto the ground. The poor little thing was covered with a slimy membrane, and its swollen tongue was blocking its mouth. I was sure this calf was dead. But John gave it a quick rub and wiped the mucus from its nose. The calf started gasping for air while I looked on with mingled horror and wonder. One thing sure, I would never have to ask where calves came from again.

"Better get into the truck," said John, breaking the spell that had come over me. From the cab we watched as the heifer got up, turned slowly around and began methodically licking her first born.

A bit farther on, we came across a cow standing by herself in the bushes. As we approached, she walked away from us, and we could see the swelled-up head of her dead calf bobbing and swinging behind her.

"What do we do now?" I asked faintly.

"We go to work again," said John grimly, "that's what we do. Damn it, why didn't I bring a saddle horse instead of this truck!"

"Shall we drive home and get one?"

He shook his head. "No time. We'll *have* to use the truck, and you'll have to drive."

"Drive where?" I asked, dreading the answer.

"After the cow. You bring the truck up close to her so I can toss a rope."

We roared across the rough field in pursuit. When she saw us coming, the cow broke into an awkward run. Every time I got near her she would turn away. Soon she was going in ever-diminishing circles, and the truck was almost spinning around. John tried to rope her, but I couldn't get in close enough for him to throw properly. I was afraid I would hit the cow—that John would fall out on his head, or that I would wreck the truck.

"Get closer, Gertie!" he yelled, and I caught the impatience in his tone.

The next time I tried, the cow stopped dead in her tracks and started in another direction. Finally, John leaped off the back of the truck and ran after the tiring animal. As I watched helplessly, he managed to snag her two hind feet and brought her down. Then I drove up, and John tied his lariat onto the back bumper. He told me to ease the vehicle forward so as to keep the rope taut—just as I'd had to do with his horse last fall.

When the cow was secure, I jumped out of the truck and ran over. John already had his arms wrapped around the calf's head and was trying to pull the body out. Although he tugged as hard as he could, the calf would not budge.

"I can't even find the damn legs," he grunted.

I got down on my knees beside him so I could get a better look. Then I wished I hadn't, for as I watched his arm disappear into the cow, I felt sick at the stomach. Every groan the cow gave started a sympathetic reaction in me.

"Isn't there some quick way we can get it out so she won't have to suffer so?" I agonized.

John shook his head. "That calf is imbedded right in her hip. It won't move an inch. Tell you what, you hold her head and I'll have a try at cutting it off."

"CUTTING IT OFF?" I was so shocked I jumped to my feet. Surely I hadn't heard him right.

"That's what I said," he nodded.

"But people don't go around cutting things that . . . well, they just don't, that's all. And if you think I'm going to touch that head, you're crazy!"

I could see John was beginning to get mad at me, but I didn't care. As I looked at the swollen head with its cold, blue nose and dangling tongue, I was sure I would faint dead away if I laid a hand on it.

"Aw come on!" said John, trying to shame me into it.

"For God's sake what's the matter with you? Do you want this cow to die when we could easily save her? And you thought you could be a nurse!"

When he put it that way, I *did* feel ashamed of myself. And I certainly didn't want the cow to die.

"Well, I'll try," I quavered. "What do you want me to do?"

"Just get that head between your knees and hold it steady while I cut," he said quietly.

"But it will be cold and clammy . . . "

"Never mind, just do it!"

I knelt down and reached out timidly to touch the head with a couple of fingers. It *was* cold and clammy! I jerked my hand away and jumped back as if I half-expected the thing to bite. This was one job I knew that I was never going to be able to do. I could get used to crowds of people, to unruly cars and even more unruly horses—even to Pop. But this . . . this was much too much.

"I just can't touch it!" I wailed.

"Gertie," said John impatiently, "there isn't any time to lose. Now come on, let's get going!"

I bent over and took another look at the proposition. It didn't look any better than the first time. But there must be worse things than having to hold a dead calf's head, I told myself. And if it meant the mother's life . . .

I knelt down again and took up the position John indicated. When I got that awful head between my knees the coldness shot up through my whole body. I shivered and shuddered. Shutting my eyes tightly, I gripped the head with both hands. John got out his hunting knife and began to cut through the muscle and bone of the calf's neck. Every time the head jarred I jumped. Suddenly, the head came off and I fell over, still holding it in my hands. I took one look at that lolling tongue and dropped it like a hot poker.

Once he had the head out of the way, John had more room to work inside the cow. It was a long struggle, with John grunting, the cow groaning and me trying to hold on to my last meal. (And right then, I was sure it *would* be my last meal). Finally, John was able to get the front legs out and the calf came free. With my stomach still reeling, I headed toward the truck.

A few nights later we had a spring blizzard. When we got up next morning, snow was still whirling merrily across the valley. But to a cattleman, a snow storm during calving is not a merry occasion. It spells trouble with a capital T. As soon as it grew light, we loaded milk, bottles, whisky, tea-spoons and our lunches into the truck's cab so we could spend the whole day in the calving field. This time, John jumped his horse into the back of the truck.

From morning until night we drove through the deepening snow. As we came to calves that had been born during the storm, we picked them up and put them into the warm cab.

"How do you know which calf belongs to which cow?" I wondered.

"Cows are just like people," John explained. "There are no two that look exactly alike."

While John drove, I dried off each new arrival, giving it a teaspoon of whiskey and some milk from a bottle. I was sort of a one-shot wet nurse. When the calf warmed up a little, we took it back to its mother and left it standing beside her to get its first suck. We had two or three calves in the cab with us all the time, messing and urinating. Naturally, I didn't have much of an appetite when lunch hour rolled around, especially when it had to be eaten in the truck.

One time we passed a cow that was busily tending to her new calf. She kept licking the little fellow—starting at the bottom and licking right up to the top of its head with big long swipes of her pink tongue.

John nodded approvingly. "Now that's what I like to see—a mother who takes her job seriously."

Some mothers give their young ones too much attention. A few minutes later, we passed a cow standing all alone by a line fence.

"I'm sure she had a calf when we came by before," John said. "Now where in hell did the little critter go? I don't see any fresh coyote tracks around here."

"You just think she had a calf," I told him. "After all, we've been looking at cows all day."

He shook his head stubbornly. "Like I said, no two cows look exactly alike. There just has to be a calf here some-where!"

Jumping out of the truck, John climbed the fence and began to look around. Soon I saw him bend down and start to pull at something. In a moment he returned with the missing calf in his arms. Its mother's long, hard licks had sent it through the fence and into a badger hole. Although the little thing had become chilled, it soon revived in the warmth of the cab.

Our next maternity case was a cow with part of her calf-bed hanging out. This meant John would need to perform a bit of an operation.

"We'll have to sew her up," he said, stopping the truck.

"Out here?" I gulped.

He shook his head. "Over there," and pointed to the distant corral. "You drive the truck, and I'll herd her along with my horse."

I watched John push the calf-bed back inside the cow, and my stomach didn't turn over once. I even squatted beside him and cut off lengths of binder twine for him to use as stitches, while he made holes for those stitches with his jack-knife in the cow's hide.

As darkness neared, we found a calf whose mother had died. While we were warming the orphan in the cab, John drove back to where he had spotted a cow standing by her dead calf.

"We'll try to get her to adopt this one," he explained.

To my consternation, he jumped out of the truck, knife in hand, and began to skin the dead calf. Then he took the orphan from the cab and draped the hide over its back, securing it with binder twine which he tied under the calf's belly. Next, he carried the struggling orphan to the cow, and we watched her sniff at it. Finally she claimed it for her own. We left the calf sucking greedily and we headed home, happy in the knowledge of a long, hard job well done.

I figured whatever formal sex education I may have gleaned from eavesdropping on my father and the vet had now been completed in the informal atmosphere of that calving field. But there was more to come. In June I began to have a few dizzy spells, so John drove me into Medicine Hat to see the doctor. That good man told me I was going to have a baby.

When I told John's youngest sister, Edith, that I was expecting, I learned that this possibility had already been thoroughly discussed by the family.

"Well, it's about time," Edith said. "Pop's been worrying about it ever since you got married. Why only the other day he was pacing about the house saying, "Hasn't he got that girl bred yet?""

I stared at Edith in shocked silence for a moment. My face turned as crimson as a prairie sunset.

"Why . . . that's a terrible thing to say!" I finally blurted.

"I guess Pop's been around cows too long," Edith laughed.

From the first day the news was out, no one doubted that we would have a son, or that we would call him John. Pop and his wife had had seven daughters before their only son was born. But somehow we all knew that John and I were not going to repeat that performance.

On a frosty morning in October, four of us headed out through the Sandhills in an open-topped army truck, bound for Medicine Hat to visit the doctor. Dode Minor, John's cousin, was driving, and Pop was beside him. John and I rode in the back seat where we could enjoy the full benefit of the nippy fall air. After we had endured the twenty miles of dips and dives which mark the trail between the ranch and the highway, Pop decided we should cut across country like they used to in the old days.

"Highways are for sissies!" he bellowed. "We were better off when we didn't have any!"

So away we went, bouncing through the hills. We scraped our way over clumps of sage and juniper, stood on our nose as we dipped into ditches and coulees, crossed countless trails, drove through fences and ploughed over sloughs and marshes—always seeking the old landmarks that Pop remembered.

"Over there!" he would shout, happily charting our course above the roar of the laboring engine. "If you round that hill there you'll find the trail we used to drive our cattle into Maple Creek!"

Dode would turn the wheel obediently and head in that direction, only to find that the trail had blown over years earlier. But Pop was undaunted. As the memories of long-forgotten trail rides came flooding back, the old man would suddenly start cussing some long-departed "son-of-a-bitch" for something that had happened during a drive fifty years ago.

Meanwhile, John was busy trying to hold me down so I wouldn't get bounced around too much. Many times our meanderings landed us in front of a fence which had no gate. This meant John and I had to alight, unstaple the wire, hold the fence down while Dode drove over it and then re-staple it.

Twice we landed in a slough and became stuck. While John and Dode struggled with the car, Pop would be on a nearby hilltop scouting the countryside. Maybe he was looking for Indians!

Finally, the absurdity of our situation caught up with us, and John and I started laughing. Here we were—with a perfectly good car sitting in the garage at home and a smooth road running all the way to the 'Hat—bouncing over the prairie in a rough old army truck. We were exposed to the chill wind, and every twist and turn meant a struggle to hold me down so I wouldn't lose our baby. Yet with all the miseries of that wild ride, I began to develop an appreciation of Pop's pioneer background, and even a little understanding of his rough ways.

We arrived at our destination about three hours behind schedule—tired and dirty. And I was far more in need of a doctor than when I left home.

Back home I began to worry a lot during the following weeks. Perhaps I was still suffering the effects of that rough trip to Medicine Hat, or maybe it was because Pop seemed to be slowing down and giving more responsibility to John. Then John began to spend a lot of his time with Jim and Minor Murray, who owned a flying service at the 'Hat. Next thing I knew, he was talking about getting a plane for the ranch.

"Easier to spot cattle when you're up in the air," he said.

The first mention of it sent danger signals shooting down into the pit of my stomach. Vigorously I fought the idea. But the more we argued, the more convinced I became that there was no talking John out of it.

As soon as Christmas was over, he took me back to Medicine Hat to await the arrival of our son. We were there in plenty of time, for little John waited until February 13th, 1946 to make his noisy debut. "Meanwhile, back at the ranch," as they say in Western stories, the baby's father had become a pilot.

Chapter VII:

Planely Speaking

With a new son and his first solo flight all in one week, John was so elated his feet hardly touched the ground. When he wasn't flying, he was sneaking in the back door of the hospital to see me. He pampered me with flowers, chocolates and special duty nurses.

When it was time for me to leave, John told me he had arranged for Jim Murray to fly us home in Jim's four-seater plane. This announcement just about sent me into a coma.

"Why, that's a crazy idea!" I cried. "What do you want to do, kill us all?"

"It's the safest way to go," he maintained stoutly. "There's nobody up there to crash into."

"There's the Law of Gravity," I told him. "Everything that goes up has to come down."

John spent many hours at the hospital and later, at Aunt Flora's, trying to convince me of the safety of air travel. It didn't make any sense to me. John had been cautious enough to drag me to Medicine Hat two months before the baby was due, and now he wanted to run the risk of killing us all.

As soon as I was up and around, he took me to the airport to see Jim's plane. Jim explained about the elaborate safety precautions and mechanical check-ups involved before a plane took off. He might have saved his breath for I didn't believe a word of it. But I had now been away two months and was anxious to get home with my little son. And I could see that the only way I was going to get there was in this flimsy-looking airplane. Against my better judgment, I agreed.

The single-engined plane stood waiting for us on the runway. It surely didn't look very safe to me, no matter what John said. Somewhere I had read that twin-engined planes were better. What a bad time to start remembering such things, I told myself. As I mounted the step into the machine's back seat, I started praying. Jim Murray insisted that I do up my seat belt. How was this going to help me when one of the wings fell off, I wondered.

Suddenly the engine burst into life and we began to move down the runway—slowly at first, then faster and faster. The engine roar deepened and the ground started to fly past at a dizzy rate. I was sure the whole thing was going to blow up. Before I could yell at them to take me back, we parted with the ground, leaving my stomach far behind. I clung to my baby, closed my eyes and prayed again—oh how I prayed!

During that seemingly endless journey, I stared blankly ahead. John was smiling and looking out the window. Every once in a while, he would point at familiar landmarks.

"See, over there!" he cried, "that's where the Red Deer joins the South Saskatchewan!"

To me, nothing seemed familiar from the air, even when I got up enough courage to look. In moments of supreme daring, I glanced quickly out the window, turning my eyes sideways without moving my head an inch. That was enough for me. Who cared where the two rivers joined. I had no desire to do any aerial sightseeing.

John swung around in his seat and drew the blanket gently from the baby's face so he could look at his son. Little John was sleeping peacefully, smiling a little.

"See, he really likes it!" John beamed. "This kid will be able to fly a plane before he learns to walk!"

"He will *not!*" I snapped. I had agreed to this trip, but that was *it* as far as I was concerned. Shuddering, I wrapped the baby up again and held him tightly. For some reason, I felt very depressed.

Every time the whine of the plane's engine changed pitch, I was certain it was going to quit on us, and every time the machine shook I shivered. At any moment I expected it to come apart in mid-flight. But to my amazement, none of these certainties came to pass.

Soon we were circling over the main ranch. The roar of

the motor lessened as we came in to land. I felt a sense of relief as the good earth came up to meet us, not knowing that this is one of the most hazardous moments of flying. Next thing I knew, we were bumping over a grassy field. When the door of the plane was opened, Pop was there to take the baby from me and carry him tenderly into the house. It was then I caught a look on the old man's face I had never seen there before—a mixture of love and tenderness and pride. For the first time, I began to see that Pop Minor was really not such a terrifying person after all.

Although Pop's house at the main ranch had no modern conveniences, it was much better than ours, so we decided to stay there until spring. As far as Pop was concerned, if you got along without something in the pioneer days you could get along without it forever. Any comfort developed since that time was senseless pampering. But John tossed this philosophy out the window the day he brought his son home. Even though lots of newborn babies had survived in the old house with only the heat from three coal and wood stoves, John decided this wasn't good enough for *his* son. While in Medicine Hat he had purchased an oil burner and had it shipped to the ranch with special instructions to his cousin Dode to have the thing working when we arrived home.

"Did you get that oil burner set up?" was his first question as we were walking from the plane to the house.

Dode shook his head. "Pop said he wasn't going to have that son-of-a-bitchin' contraption in his house. He says he's lived here fifty years and raised nine children, and what was good enough for him is good enough for you folks."

"Oh, he did, eh?" said John, and I saw his face beginning to set the way it had when we were arguing about the airplane.

By this time, we had reached the front porch, and there was the oil burner still sitting in the crate it had been shipped in.

John didn't even stop to remove his coat. He grabbed a hammer and began to knock the crate apart. Leaving the wood strewn all over the porch, he and Dode dragged the new burner into the dining room.

Pop stuck his shaggy head out of the lower bedroom.

"You're not setting that son-of-a-bitch up in here!" he bellowed.

John paid no attention. Without saying a word, he strode over to the coal and wood heater in the center of the dining room and methodically began to tear it apart—in spite of the fact it was still hot from the dying embers inside. Pop didn't say anymore, but he showed his displeasure by stomping from the room, whistling that dry little whistle of his.

Smoke billowed from the hot stove as John and Dode finished dismantling it. Soon we were all gasping and choking, but that didn't stop them. A trail of ashes followed them across the floor as they dragged the thing through the door and heaved it out the back. From around a corner, Pop gazed in dismay at the fate of this old friend he had stoked and poked for fifty years.

As always, when John decided to do something he just did it. I thought he might have been a bit more tactful with his father. After all, it is harder to accept change as you grow older.

John just laughed when I suggested this. "Heck, in a few days you won't be able to pry him away from that oil stove."

As it turned out, he knew his father a lot better than I did. Soon Pop was back in the dining room, standing silently behind John and Dode as they wrestled the oil burner into position. Next thing I knew, he was telling them how to fit the pieces of pipe together. When they finally got the stove working, he was the first to warm his hands over it.

Pop stayed awake most of that night for fear this new contraption would blow up. But when morning came and the house was still intact, he emerged smiling from his bedroom. The dining room was warm, he had one less fire to light and one less pailful of ashes to carry out.

In the spring, John decided to dismantle the oil burner so we could take it back to our place with us, but Pop protested.

"I'm getting kind of used to that son-of-a-bitch," he said. "You'd better order another one."

We ordered two—one for ourselves, and another one to heat the other side of Pop's house. The oil burner's arrival signified a new era at the Minor Ranch. We decided to modernize the whole operation. The next step was a more dramatic one. John made up his mind to buy an airplane.

Pop—who by nature opposed any innovation—just about blew his stack. Buying a plane was the craziest thing he had ever heard of. As usual, he said so in no uncertain terms.

"If we'd been meant to ranch that way they never would've invented horses!" he shouted.

John explained how much easier and better this big ranch could be run with an airplane, but the old man would have none of it.

"I've been running this place for fifty years," he snorted, "and I never needed any goddam plane!"

John sighed resignedly. He knew he would have to buy the plane from his own personal savings—the same way he had bought the oil burner. This time, however, he would have to dig up a lot more money. I opposed the purchase of the plane too. My position was that it would be much too dangerous to have him up flying every day of the year, and that we had more important things to spend our money on.

As usual, there was no stopping John once he was certain his idea was sound. I think both Pop and I realized this as soon as John broached the idea. We knew we were fighting a hopeless rearguard action.

The secondhand, single-engined J-3 arrived at the ranch on a clear April day. When John landed, everyone gathered around the machine to inspect it. All except Pop, that is. He stood away from the others, silent and stony-faced. Every line of his body showed his disapproval.

"Come on, Pop!" John shouted. I'll take you up for a ride!"

"The hell you will!" the old man bellowed. "You couldn't get me into that son-of-a-bitchin' thing for a million dollars!" Then he turned and walked briskly toward the house and we heard that tell-tale whistle again.

Most of those first days I went about my work with my eyes half-turned toward that great expanse of prairie sky. When I wasn't working I would be pacing up and down in front of our living room window. And I kept on worrying until John had landed safely. Each time he came in he regaled me with enthusiastic details of how the ranch looked

Pop Minor came to Canada in 1900. This photo, taken in 1903, shows
Pop with the skin of a gray wolf he had shot.

This ranch house, built in 1916, was the home of Mr. and Mrs. John Minor I. It was here that author Gertrude Minor came as a bride.

Abbey, Saskatchewan, 1912. Author born here in 1926.

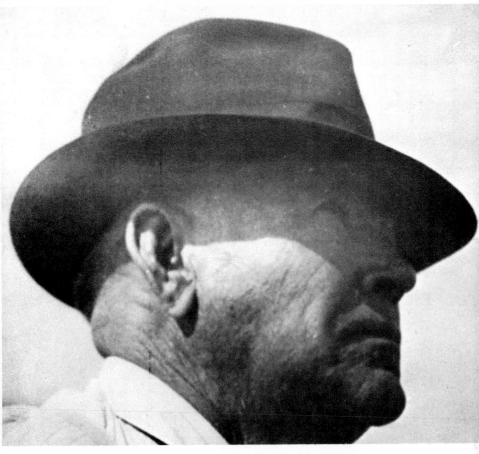

Pop Minor in 1939. Gruff on the outside, tender on the inside.

The Pioneers of the Great Sandhills. Frank Yeast, Sr., Sam Anderson, Sr., John Minor, Sr., and Mr. Milly, Sr.

Pop Minor and son John, 1934. ("Stand up like you got corn to sell!"). After seven daughters, Pop finally got a son.

Two cowboys, Pop Minor and son John.

Gertrude Minor in 1947 with her son John.

Gertrude Minor preparing the branding dinner, the big event of the year. Over 150 people would show up for dinner.

The cooks for the 1955 branding dinner. Mrs. Dode Minor, Gertrude Minor, Mrs. Frank Yeast and Mrs. Dode Minor, Sr.

Branding day, 1957. John Minor II on the right.

The Minor Ranch farm buildings located at the edge of the Great Sandhills in Saskatchewan. John and Katherine Minor raised their nine children in this home. The big barn burned down in 1964.

John Minor II with his first airplane. Plane served also as the Sandhills
Air Ambulance.

Chilco Ranch, 1962. John Minor, Wally Wells, Ken McKnight and Lee
Brooks.

Chilco Ranch. John Minor ready for take off. 1962.

After an animal was artificially inseminated, John Minor put on a number brand for the records.

Choosing the bull for the day, Murrell Bowman (left) a veterinary student from Guelph, Ontario, and John Minor. Note semen chest where semen was stored in dry ice and alcohol.

Rex Bovee cutting out an aproned bull from the cows.

John was happiest when he was out riding with his family.

John and Gertie Minor with children John, Ross, Barry and Susan.

John Minor II.

Chilco Ranch, 1963

Chilco Ranch house.

Chilco Ranch house. John Minor III (left) and Lorence Willness.

Storing semen in liquid nitrogen was a safer and more convenient method.

Our wagon train boss, Eggie Elkink, his wife Kay, plus John and Gertrude Minor.

Chilco Ranch store where everything from a needle to a wagon was sold.

Christmas Day, 1962. Chilco Ranch store goes up in flames.

Young John's birthday, February, 1963. Chilco Ranch.

Getting ready to put dehorning paste on calves.

Barry Minor is present owner of the Home Valley Ranch.

John Minor III.

One of the many brandings at Home Valley. Sandhills in the background.

John Minor III slapping on brand used for three generations. Asa Yeast holding the head and Jim Braaten in the foreground.

Blazing wood fire is no longer used for heating branding irons. Propane torch is now preferred. John Minor III (center) and Alec Watson.

Daughter Susan Minor shows roping isn't just for the guys.

The art of calf wrestling continues with each generation as Barry Minor works over calf as his daughters Kelly and Carrie hang on tight.

Tomorrow's breakfast, "Prairie Oysters." The bucket is still carried around by a young recruit as each calf is castrated.

Trail Ride sponsored by the Saskatchewan Stock Growers Association.

Home Valley Ranch, home of Barry Minor and family. 1000 head of steers ready to go under the hammer.

from above and of how fast he could check over the whole operation by plane.

"Man, it gives you a free-and-easy feeling when you're soaring around up there!" he would say.

But he could never get me to agree to go with him, no matter how he tried to sell me on the idea. Flying was "strictly for the birds," and to me this was more than just a popular expression. I was terrified of it.

Finally, about a week after the plane's arrival, I faced up to the problem. I was preparing for another day of pacing and worrying when I suddenly thought to myself, "What's the sense going on like this? If he's going to get killed, I might as well get killed too." Without giving myself time for any further thinking, I told our hired girl to look after the baby, followed John out to the machine and climbed in. He didn't say anything but he looked pleased.

As expected, I did not enjoy the flight, but it was a lot less nerve-wracking than worrying about John from below.

Next day, John was busy warming up the plane when out walked Pop from the front of the house. With determined steps, he headed for the machine and climbed into the back seat—all without saying a single word. They circled slowly over the buildings a couple of times, then headed toward the hills on John's daily check of cattle, windmills and fences. In less than half an hour they were back, having done a job that would take a couple of fence riders all day. Pop was beaming broadly as he climbed from the plane.

"Yes sir," he said, "that's quite an outfit we've got there!"

Strutting over to a group of his men working nearby, he began to brag about all he had seen. You would think the whole idea of getting the plane had been his alone.

"Why, you can even see the goddam brands on those cattle!" he finished, with a look of satisfaction.

By this time, I was beginning to *want* to go up in the plane, but now my opportunities were few and far between. As soon as Pop heard the machine start up, he would run out of the house and jump in. No matter how I tried I could never beat him to it.

The plane became John's constant companion. His flying day began before breakfast, when he would go up just so he

65

could catch the full beauty of the awakening day. As he predicted, the machine proved to be a big timesaver, leaving him time to consider other projects and activities. He flew to where he was working each day, both to save precious time and to have the machine available so he could fly into town for repairs whenever any equipment broke down.

Besides the daily check of the whole operation, John saw he could use the plane to spot cows in trouble during the calving season, to round up the cattle for branding day by chasing them in toward the windmill where the riders picked them up, and to take lunches and messages out to the distant locations where the men were working. More than anything else, the plane pushed the Minor Ranch into the efficiency-oriented twentieth century. In this case, it hadn't taken much pushing, for John was crazy to fly.

One windy August day John was haying near the farm when a black, black cloud appeared over the horizon. Suddenly remembering that the plane was only lightly tied down, John and one of his men jumped into a truck and rushed for the airstrip. But the dust storm was already upon them. As they struggled to turn the little craft into the wind, they were struck with a blast which tossed the machine about thirty feet into the air. The next moment it came crashing back to earth, a total wreck.

"Well," said John later, as he slumped dejectedly into a kitchen chair, "you didn't want me to have a plane, and I haven't got one, so I guess you'll be happy now."

"What happened?"

"The wind smashed it. Picked it up and tossed it on the ground like an angry kid would break a toy."

"I'm sorry," was all I could think to say. And I really meant it, for now that the machine was smashed I realized what a handy thing it was to have around the place.

We knew it was useless to think about buying another. Our total savings had gone into buying that one.

Next morning at five a.m. Pop came roaring through the hills in the old army truck. "JOHN!" he shouted, as he stomped into our kitchen, "You'd better order another one of those goddam flying machines. We need it around here!"

We could hardly believe our ears. John was the first to recover. "I sure will!" he beamed.

66

Within a few days he was off to Oshawa, Ontario, to pick up a new Piper Super Cub.

Later that year I became ill soon after returning home from the hospital where I had been recovering from a miscarriage. John wanted to rush me back to the doctor right away, but I assured him it was nothing but an attack of flu. Things went on like this for three days, with John trying to convince me to go to the doctor and me insisting there was nothing seriously wrong. Finally, John got so worried he phoned my sister, Evelyn, who is a nurse.

"Never mind what she says," Evelyn told him, "you get her to the doctor as fast as you can. It sounds to me like she's got blood poisoning. Our mother died of that you know."

I remember John carrying me to the plane and strapping me into the back seat. That was the last thing I was to remember for three days. John radioed Medicine Hat to have an ambulance waiting at the airport when we arrived. Had we been an hour later, it would have been too late.

The hospital was the same one where John had spent so much time trying to coax me to take my first flight. As I lay there now, I had plenty of time to consider how fortunate I was to have a husband who was a pilot, and that we had an airplane. Although I had made my case as difficult as possible, the plane had saved my life. My fears about the machine disappeared. It was a vital part of our ranch operation now and I wouldn't have it otherwise.

That was our plane's first ambulance mission—the first of many, many more. During the following winter, roads in our area were blocked for days on end with drifting snow. In the middle of his busy schedule—no matter what the weather was like—John would answer distress calls from people who had to get to the hospital in a big hurry.

I remember three days in particular. In the middle of a howling blizzard, John picked up a woman who was going to have a baby. He flew her into the hospital at Cabri, twenty miles southeast of Abbey, in plenty of time for the birth. Then he headed for home, happy in the knowledge he had helped a neighbor in need.

The second day, he received a frantic call from a father-to-be on a farm near Shackleton, about ten miles due east. When John arrived to pick up the mother, he found the house in a turmoil. It was too late to move the woman, and her husband—clad only in a fur hat and a pair of long-johns—was running around in confusion as he tried to get things ready.

"I've gotta get a kettle—a big kettle," he kept repeating.

In spite of his agitation, the man was able to tell John that a doctor was already on his way from Cabri so the baby could be delivered right here in the house.

John jumped into his plane and flew down the road until he spotted the doctor's car. Landing well ahead of the vehicle, he flagged the doctor down, helped him into the plane and took off for the farm. True to the tradition of the old west, the doctor arrived in the nick of time to save the perspiring father and deliver a bouncing baby girl.

But sometimes even a western tradition can fall by the wayside. The next day was bitterly cold, with the yellow sundogs pacing a pale gold sun across the sky. It was a good day to stay inside and toast your feet beside a roaring fire, and John would have done just that if we hadn't received a distress call from an expectant mother near Lancer, a few miles to the northwest.

When John saw the woman, he was sure it was too late to move her. He was becoming a bit of an expert on the frequency of birth pains by this time. "Are you sure you should be going, ma'am?" he asked.

"Aw, it took me hours to have my other kids," she told him confidently. "Don't give it another thought."

Three thousand feet in the air, and about half the distance to the Cabri hospital, John was forced to think of it again when the woman suddenly yelled, "Hey, I'm going to have the baby!"

Then the windows began to fog up so that John had to open a door to see where he was going. With the 20-below-zero air streaming into the cab of the plane, the mother called desperately: "I'm having it... I'm having it!" and she fainted dead away.

John did not panic. There was nothing he could do but keep flying and get the woman to the hospital as quickly as possible. (Laughing about it later, he said it's easy to keep cool when the temperature is 20-below.)

In a few minutes, the exhausted mother regained

consciousness.

"The baby's here!" she announced.

"Good!" John shouted over his shoulder. "But for God's sake wrap it up and keep it warm!"

In Cabri, he landed the plane right beside the hospital and charged inside where he encountered two startled nurses.

"I've got a woman in my plane who has just had a baby!" he told them. "You'd better call the doctor and get me some blankets!"

When they still stared at him in disbelief, he repeated it, and added, "I'll need blankets to wrap around her until the doctor comes."

Still in a daze, they produced some blankets, and shoved them toward John. Rushing out to the plane, he wrapped the blankets around the woman and child. Then the doctor ran up, carrying his little black bag. In that 20-below wind, with John passing the instruments, the doctor set calmly to work. When they were finished, they transferred the patients to the hospital. Both mother and child came through that harrowing experience with no ill effects at all.

When John reached home, he swaggered into the house wearing an impish grin.

"Well, Gertie," he chuckled, "this is one time I didn't make it."

"What do you mean?" I asked.

"She had it in the back of the plane."

"Oh, you're kidding!" I laughed, and walked out of the room.

"If you don't believe it," he yelled after me, "come on out and help me clean up the back of the cab!"

I believed it all right when we had to spend the rest of the day chiseling away at the frozen afterbirth. I had come a long way from the little girl who wondered where calves came from each spring!

Chapter VIII:

Not One Damn Word

During the first few years of our marriage, it seemed that we were constantly moving back and forth between our place and the main ranch. If Pop took sick—if his hired girl quit—or if Pop happened to be short of men, we had to move in with him until things got straightened out.

While we were there, I always felt that uneasiness which comes with living in someone else's house. I was not so afraid of Pop now, but I was afraid *for* him. His health was beginning to fail, and I worried that I was not doing enough to help him. At the same time I didn't want to do too much on my own for fear he would think I was trespassing on his domain. The result was that I never felt at home and I had to contend with far more visitors than we had at our place. Every summer the house was chuck full of family and friends and the household in a constant state of disruption.

The only way I could keep my health and sanity was to stick to a rigid schedule. Every day we would clean the house from attic to basement, serve hot, full-course meals on the dot at six a.m., noon and six p.m. I would also bake all the bread and buns needed, churn the butter, ensure there were lots of pies and cakes for desserts, put the children to bed at a set hour each night and then "relax" with a pile of washing, ironing or mending. Part of this routine was absolutely necessary to keep our large crew of ranch hands satisfied, the rest was just the Scottish engineer in me. Everything had to run like clockwork or I would become too frustrated to live with.

One thing which bothered us was that we were never alone. Everytime we tried to go anywhere, about a dozen boisterous children would pile into the back of our car. They loved to be with us because we were young and happy. We accepted it all in a light, carefree manner, although there were times when we longed to escape the crowds and get back to our little home in the hills. And as soon as circumstances permitted, we did.

We were living at our own place in October, 1947, when John flew me home with our second son, Ross. As we landed near the house, I could see that John had been busy in my absence. He had built a new fence around the yard as a surprise for our homecoming. But the biggest surprise was inside. There were new electric lights, a propane stove and a new washing machine. That's why I was so sad when, about four months later, we loaded our furniture into a truck and left our house forever.

This time, Pop was very ill and the couple who had been looking after him were leaving. We had always known that some day we would have to take over at the main ranch. It was as inevitable as the wind blowing across the grasslands. Now that the day arrived, John decided he would move his family in properly—bringing all our possessions and fixing up the house to suit our needs. I dreaded the conflicts I knew would be forthcoming. But the first assault on our new territory turned out be more violent than I expected.

It was evening when the men began unloading our furniture from the truck. As usual, I was in a stew. I was trying vainly to keep them from tracking in too much snow, supervising the placing of furniture and boxes and trying to put my two sons to bed. On top of it all I had a first-class mental conflict going as I tried to reconcile myself to the idea that we were really here to stay. Then, over the banging of furniture, the scuffling of wet boots, the crying of the baby and the pounding of my thoughts, I heard a thundering crash from the den. The noise continued—in fact, it got louder and louder. Gosh, what now? I asked myself, as I ran to investigate.

To my horror, I found John—still clad in his winter hat and wet overshoes—methodically wielding a big axe on the lath and plaster wall which separated the den from his father's bedroom.

"John, what are you doing?" I screamed. "Have you

gone crazy?" Even as I spoke, plaster dust and thin, narrow strips of wood flew in every direction. A choking white film filled the room and settled all over the furniture.

"Just making a few changes," he said calmly. "We're going to have a new bathroom."

"Do you *have* to do it tonight?" I choked.

"If I don't do it now, we'll never be able to do it," he said, without even missing a stroke of his axe.

"Did you talk it over with Pop?"

"He knows about it," John nodded. "He said we could make any changes we liked."

Looking behind him, I saw Pop standing in the middle of the den, watching the demolition in silent resignation. As clearly as if he had spoken, his eyes said, "I'm going to have to let him do this or he and Gertie won't stay." All at once I realized what a terrible thing it was for a man as forceful as Pop to get old and have to be so dependent on others. My heart went out to him.

"How about coming into the kitchen and I'll make you a cup of cocoa," I suggested.

"Nope," he said. "If I don't stay here he's liable to keep right on going and we'll find ourselves sleeping in the snow."

Pop did not accept the actual installation of the bathroom quite as calmly. He watched the carpenter at work for awhile in stony silence, then he announced to the whole family: "I wouldn't use that thousand-dollar shithouse for anybody!" and stomped off with something of his old spirit.

John winked at me. "He must be feeling better," he said with a grin.

Although the bathroom adjoined Pop's new bedroom, he tried to ignore it. For the first few days, he stubbornly trekked out through the winter snowbanks to his beloved outdoor facility. Then one day, we saw him sneak in and out of the new bathroom when he thought we weren't looking. For our benefit, he still made a few trips outside, but even these stopped when he realized we knew he had weakened.

The place where Pop bothered me most was in the kitchen. And he was in it a good deal of the time because he had been relieved of just about all the ranch work.

"My mother died early so I learned to cook when I was a

little shaver," he would tell me for about the umpteenth time. "'Twas my grandmother who taught me. She was blind, you know. The rest of it I got the hard way—cooking for the whole goddam crew on the oldtime chuckwagon roundups. They were a hard bunch, and they liked their grub just so."

"Just so it wasn't burnt too bad," another oldtimer chuckled when I was telling him about it years later.

Pop believed that no one could organize a kitchen the way he could. And he was right. No one could, or would. Everything he cooked was extra rich, and I longed to tell him that he might be able to skip his frequent attacks of indigestion if he used less butter. But it was his kitchen, so I figured I had to do things his way. I relieved my frustrations by making a private list of all Pop's kitchen practices which annoyed me. It was as long as a shadow at sundown.

My biggest peeve was the pan of fried onions which Pop insisted on serving for breakfast three times a week. I was the one who had to peel those tearful tidbits and start them frying. Then our master chef would come along and pour water into the pan. This was not the way I thought onions should be cooked, but I was so used to keeping my thoughts to myself by now that I said nothing.

One summer morning in 1948 Pop failed to turn up at his usual hour. This should have put me in a bright mood, but little John, now two years old, and Ross, who was nine months, were playing under my feet so that I had to watch my step every moment. I was also a bit edgy because I was expecting another baby in January and the smell of freshly-peeled onions that early in the morning did nothing to improve my temper. If I could just get those onions fried my way before Pop arrived, I told myself, I might be able to get through the rest of the day without going crazy.

With one eye on the door, I flew from onion bag-to-peeler-to-pot-to-stove in a frenzy. While rushing around like that, I caught the pocket of my apron on the handle of the frying pan. As I turned to leave the stove, away went the pan, strewing greasy onions across the floor. "If he comes in now, I might as well give up," I muttered. "This is all he'll need to convince himself he's indispensible in the kitchen."

Down on my hands and knees I went, taking desperate

swipes at the linoleum with my cloth in a panic to get the mess cleaned up before Pop appeared on the scene. As I wiped a path across the room, I came upon two slipper-shod feet planted firmly in the middle of the floor. I didn't have to look up to know who was standing there. A wave of anger began to rise in me. If it weren't for this rough old man I wouldn't be in such a mess—in fact, I wouldn't even be cooking onions. Tears of frustration cascaded down my cheeks.

Looking up at his solid figure, all my restraint suddenly broke: "Not one damn word from you!" I cried. "Do you hear?"

The look on Pop's face was a sight to see. Concern changed to amusement and then to undisguised delight. His daughter-in-law had finally stood up to him as he had been hoping she would all along.

"Had a little tough luck, eh girl?" he said kindly, then he went out of the room humming happily to himself.

At that moment I grew up. For suddenly I realized Pop liked me more now than he ever had, and the reason he liked me was that I had finally stood up for myself. With shame, I recalled those countless times I had buried my feelings in order not to cross him, when all along he had never wanted me—or anyone else—to cower before him. Nor would he ever really respect anyone who did.

It's true that over the years my early fear of Pop had eroded until it was half annoyance and half love—with a strong measure of respect for his strength and judgment. But I had always stopped short of exposing my feelings to him, and this had prevented any real understanding between us. Now that I had "cussed him out," as he would say, my heart was free to love him.

Chapter IX:

A Double Loss

As could be expected, John and I had quite different ideas about what was important when hiring help. John's main concern was getting the ranch work done; everything else was secondary. I worried more about the personal habits of one girl working for us. After all, I was the one who cleaned up after them, washed their clothes, put my good tablecloths in front of them and wondered about the kind of example they would set for my growing children. I also worried about what kind of tall tales they might spread about the family.

As a young girl in the community, I had always been upset when disloyal hired hands spread unkind stories about the Minors. I knew the Minors were fair to their help. After I joined the family, I was determined that no worker would be able to say I had mistreated him or her in any way. In spite of my efforts, there were inevitably those who spread stories, and when these stories reached my sensitive ears I was quite crushed.

"Now why would she say a thing like that?" I would fret.

But John just laughed at such things. "The trouble with you is that you put everyone on a pedestal," he'd say, "then when they do something that isn't right, your whole world is shattered. Don't expect too much and you won't be disappointed, I always say. Live and let live!"

Worst of all was the inside help. After many bad experiences, in 1950 we ended up with a fifteen-year-old English girl. Everyone was sure she would quit in a couple of days. She was slim, with pale skin, rosy cheeks and dark brown hair—and scared as a rabbit in a coyote den.

John brought her home just as our boisterous crew was sitting down at the long dining room table and her big brown eyes stared at the noisy scene in stark disbelief. One side of the table was filled with young hungry ranch hands. Our three little boys, ages two, three and four were noisier than usual, and our baby girl Susan, born in March, was screaming at the top of her lungs for her dinner.

Behind her, John was shaking his head, and I knew he had decided there was no hope for this one. As I watched her step timidly into that big roomful of rough men, I remembered a certain frightened bride who had felt the same way as she came into this very room about six years ago. My heart went out to her.

Pop, of course, was still acting out his role as the terror of the boondocks.

"What's your name?" he boomed at her, and the young girl trembled.

"Viola," she mumbled, but her voice was so low that Pop only half-heard.

"Gladiola?" he shouted, "Where in hell did you get a name like that?"

Everybody roared with laughter, and Viola was too intimidated to correct the error. From that day on, Pop called her "Oley" and the name stuck.

Her first year with us was a record of incompetence. But Oley had one thing the others didn't have, she *wanted* to do well. She tried so hard to please us. When we moved to the Milley place in 1950, our own holding, I decided we wouldn't need Oley, but she had other ideas.

"I'm coming whether you pay me or not," she said.

"What'll I do?" I asked John. "She wants to stay with us and I really don't need her."

"We'll take her along at her regular pay," John grinned, "She'll be all right. With four kids and a house to get ready you'll find lots of work to do."

Our patience was finally rewarded. Oley developed into one of our most efficient helpers, and we came to look on her as one of the family. And while we waited for her to learn, we harvested many chuckles and a few belly laughs. Watching her, I could only sympathize, for I had provided a few myself.

One day at the Milley place, when the men were away putting up winter feed, Oley decided she would take over the job of milking our cow. From then on, at four o'clock every morning and afternoon she marched out to the barn with grim determination. Sometimes she did return with a pail of milk, but not very often. Usually she would throw open the kitchen door about six o'clock, crash the battered, manure-spattered, empty pail onto the cupboard top and glare at me with angry eyes.

"If that's a milk cow I'm the Queen of Sheba!" she cried once. "Of all the dirty, mean, jittery, uncooperative..." and her voice trailed off in a tirade of abuse.

"I don't see why she should suddenly turn contrary," I said. "She's always had a pleasant disposition."

"Pleasant! If she's pleasant, then Hitler must have been a saint!"

Next day, I decided to sneak out to the barn during Oley's two-hour milkless vigil and see what was going on. The battle was in full swing when I arrived.

Her face an angry red, Oley was planted in front of the cow, twisting the poor critter's ears to the tempo of her measured insults. Then our volunteer milkmaid hit the cow over the head and returned to her action station at the rear. The action was not long in coming. Angrily, the cow switched her tail and caught Oley full in the face

"Darn you!" she shouted.

The sudden shout was so loud the cow jumped back nervously, knocking over the pail. This was too much for Oley. Grabbing the pail quickly, she banged it across the cow's rump. By this time, manure was flying, insults filled the air and the jittery cow was jumping back and forth in her stall. Any milk which may have been available was now well drawn up. I decided to halt the battle right there before one or the other got hurt.

"You can't force a cow," I explained to Oley. "You've got to coax her so she wants to give milk."

"She doesn't want to give anybody anything but a rough time," Oley retorted, and flounced out of the barn.

Toward spring, Oley and I, the children and one hired man were stranded at the Milley place for two weeks when a blizzard cut off all access. John couldn't even get to us with the plane. He had the machine with him at the home ranch, but its skis were with us.

The blizzard struck from the north without warning. At the fall of the first snowflake we ran out of both propane and fuel oil. Our main fuel storage tanks were several hundred yards away, but in a howling blizzard like that they might as well have been in Timbuktu. When modern means fail on the prairie the safest thing to do is return to the old ways, which we promptly did. Across the yard was an old, unused house equipped with a coal and wood stove. We could still see its outline against the driving snow so there was no danger of our getting lost. As soon as the hired man had a fire going, we moved over there for our meals. At bedtime, we carried the children through the snowdrifts to the bunkhouse where there was plenty of room to sleep.

Late that night, with everyone snugly bedded down in the new quarters, our dog started having pups. The delivery took until morning, which was about par for the course as far as ranch births are concerned. Soon the kids began to stir and we had a whole new glorious day to look forward to. And it promised to be just as stormbound as the last one!

When the hired man was able to get our fuel supply going again, we moved back into the house. In the long, lonely days which followed, the wind blew and blew, drifting deep snow across the roads and trails until we were completely sealed off from the outside world. Oley and I decided that if we didn't keep busy we'd get "cabin fever," so we started our spring housecleaning. We washed ceilings and walls and walls and ceilings until we didn't know which way was up.

By the end of our first week, the only staple food left in our cupboard was dried beans. For two meals each day in the week that followed, Oley cooked a batch of beans in the pressure cooker. Oley didn't get along any better with the pressure cooker than she had with the cow—in fact, after a long series of failures with the infernal contraption, she loathed the sight of it. Her annoyance at having to use it twice a day was compounded by having to eat beans all the time. At every encounter with either cooker or beans, she would fly into a rage.

At last came the happy day when John plowed a path

to the house, and walked through the door carrying a big bag of groceries. He almost ran into Oley who was standing in front of the bean-filled pressure cooker cursing it and all its contents in a style that would have done credit to Pop.

"What's the matter with you?" John asked mildly.

"If I see another damn bean, I'll blow up!" she yelled.

At that moment, the pressure cooker retaliated with a loud "bang!" which sent beans and bean juice cascading all over Oley's freshly-scrubbed ceiling.

By the time we moved back to the home place in the fall of 1951 because Pop had taken ill, Oley had developed into an efficient housekeeper. She could now cook an excellent meal for any number of people and serve it exactly on the dot, and God help anyone who interfered in her kitchen.

Oley's most efficient day was one New Years when she was persuaded to take her first drink and her last. She was right in the middle of preparations of a feast for forty people and downed the drink without batting an eye. Amused at the way the drink reddened her already rosy cheeks and increased the speed of her lively tongue, the men gave her another and another. Her eyes got darker and her cheeks redder, but she didn't slow down. In fact, with each drink Oley worked faster and better until she had the meal on the table ahead of schedule.

"The funny part is I didn't feel a thing," she said later in disbelief, "I just got everything done so fast!"

"As Lincoln might have said, find out what brand she uses and I'll give it to the rest of the crew," John laughed.

In spite of all she had learned, Oley still had trouble with the pressure cooker. She never seemed to be able to master the thing. Another New Year's day, I was busily stirring a pan of gravy on the stove while Oley completed preparations for dinner. The roast was in the oven, the cupboard doors were wide open, bowls and pots of hot food covered the table and stove—plum puddings were steaming merrily in the pressure cooker at my side. Unknown to me, Oley had been unable to locate the cooker's valve so she had blocked the hole with a match stick.

Suddenly there was a shattering explosion. Next thing I knew, I was in the dining room, pulling pieces of glass out of the back of my neck. Through the doorway a scene of carnage greeted my eyes. The lid from the pressure cooker had shot through the lath and plaster of the ceiling and imbedded itself in the joists overhead. Plum pudding—still dripping from above—had mingled with bits of flying glass to ruin all the prepared food on the stove and table.

But Oley wasn't worried about having to cook a whole new dinner. She was gazing ruefully at both the propane stoves. They were smashed to pieces. Just then John rushed into the kitchen, closely followed by Pop. They had heard the blast from all the way over in the bunkhouse and were sure we'd been hurt.

"All right!" Oley barked. "So I have to buy you a new stove!" Angrily she picked up the fallen stove pipes and heaved them into the sink.

John looked around quickly to assure himself that no one was hurt, then he laughed. "That's the least of our worries as long as no one is injured."

Pop, who had always looked on the cooker as just another dangerous modern gadget, assured Oley she would never have to worry about such a contraption again. Oley nodded in agreement, her black eyes blazing.

"That's the last time I'm having a son-of-a-bitchin' thing like that in my house!" he stated flatly.

Oley was with us five years, and during that time she had many a noisy battle. Now that she had mastered her job, no one could intimidate her, and Pop respected her for it.

One day, a visitor came into the kitchen when the two were arguing. "Is that your daughter?" he asked Pop.

"Hell, no!" Pop boomed. "Do you think I'd have a flat-footed Englishman like that for a daughter?"

"Any more than I'd have a terrible old man like him for a father!" she retorted, much to the visitor's amusement.

The kitchen became Oley's private domain, and she would not stand having other people interfere there, not even well-meaning ones who wanted to help. Eventually, the inevitable happened—she got married. At the reception we held at home for her, she could not control her impatience at the sight of other women in *her* kitchen. Wedding gown and all, she tried to get her hands into the dishpan, but we chased her out.

After her honeymoon, she and her husband worked for

us the rest of the summer.

How I missed her when she left, for we considered her as part of our family and loved her dearly.

Not long after Oley left, we suffered a deeper personal loss. Pop's health hadn't improved and in the summer of 1953, he died.

With his passing, a lot of the life and color went out of the Minor Ranch. You might say a ranch is just a beef production factory, and so it is. But old-timers like Pop gave it that romantic air which has followed the man on horseback since knighthood days. Whatever that romantic quality is, you will not find it in this modern world of airplanes, jeeps and trucks.

The winter of 1952-53 was a hard one for Pop. John's oldest sister Mary—who was a registered nurse—came with her two children in March to stay and look after him. Some days he was pretty low. Then he would perk up and regale us with stories of the past as his memories came trailing home.

Pop liked to hold our daughter Susan who was now three on his knee even though he was often too weak to lift her.

One day, when the two of them were sleeping in his chair, a young neighbor whose family Pop helped get started—and later helped through the agony of the Thirties—came to the door and demanded to talk to him. I could see he was very angry, and I didn't want him to upset Pop in any way.

"He's resting," I said. But this young gallant barged right on into the livingroom with his hat and overshoes on.

Going over to Pop, I shook him gently, and said there was someone to see him. As he looked up, he recognized the fellow, and his piercing blue eyes took on a quizzical look.

"You owe me a hundred dollars, Mr. Minor!" the neighbor snapped. "Your horses got into my crop."

I saw Pop stiffen, and his head shot up with a trace of his old fire. Then his body relaxed.

"Sit down, young man," he said quietly. "I want to tell you a story."

In a firm voice he began to talk of the days when this man's folks had first come to this country—how he had helped them every way possible, as he did with all that needed help, with food, money, clothing and his time, and how he had watched with disappointment when they chased their cattle into his feed ground. But he had let them remain because he knew they were out of feed, even though he was short himself.

He named many, many incidents when he had given them help. As Pop talked, the intruder sank deeper and deeper into his chair, his face as red as a field-ripened tomato.

"Now, young man," Pop finished. "How much did you say I owe you?"

Without a word, the fellow got up and sheepishly left the house.

A few days later while quietly sitting in his chair, watching the kids playing some game that ended in a quarrel with one of them promising to get even with the other, Pop's memory trailed back again.

"I was going to get even with a fellow once," he said, "a long time ago. It was when Mama, your grandmother, and I were going to get married. We started off to Maple Creek with a team and wagon. When we got across the Sandhills and into the farming country it was storming real bad. Mama was cold and the horses were played out. It was almost dark so we stopped at a farm and asked if we could spend the night. Well, they said we could but I had to sleep in the barn and they gave Mama a place in the house. The next morning I asked the man how much we owed him and he said $10, so I paid him but I vowed I'd get even with him some day if it took me the rest of my life.

"Many years later, this same man, caught in another storm, pulled into this yard and asked if he could spend the night here. 'You bet,' I said. So we helped him unharness his team and fed and watered them. We invited him in for supper and we gave him the best bed in the house to sleep in. Next morning we fed him a big breakfast and when he was ready to leave, Mama passed him a lunch to take with him. 'How much do I owe you Mr. Minor?' he asked."

"'Not a thing, neighbor,' I said. 'Not a thing.' Yes sir, I finally got even," Pop mused.

As Pop was in the house all the time now, we had many

discussions when he was feeling up to it. On the topic of religion he said, "If a person sticks to them there Ten Commandments, you can't go too far wrong in this world."

I smiled when I thought of the third one he broke quite regularly, but I realized he thought he had the priority in this case. I remembered the family telling of a young man who came to work from Toronto. After being there for a few days he made the drastic mistake of saying "damn." Pop jumped on him immediately.

"That's pretty strong language to be using around my daughters," he said. "From now on I do the cussing around here young man."

Pop was small in stature but large in generosity. His gruffness was the only protection he had from his own heart.

We looked after Pop as long as we could, but in the last week of July we had to take him to the hospital. John was with him as much as possible and toward the end, slept in the maternity room next door. Pop's eyes would have twinkled at that, had he been conscious. Then on August 3rd, 1953, Pop slipped quietly away.

As I sat at his funeral, I wondered how John would do in filling his shoes.

John responded to his father's death by throwing himself into the ranching business with even more enthusiasm and vigor than before.

His first task was to borrow money and buy his father's ranch from the estate, improving it as he went along. A few years later he bought another ranch in the Moose Mountains, stocking and improving that also.

When he wasn't involved in ranch work or his family's activities, he was attending some convention or meeting. John eventually became President of the Saskatchewan Stock Growers, First Vice-President of the Council of Canadian Beef Producers (Western Section), and in 1961 he was appointed the Sasketchewan representative on the Advisory Committee to the Agricultural Stabilization Board. Because he had pioneered the use of artificial insemination on range cattle, John was asked to speak on numerous occasions.

"Do you always have to get up so early?" I groaned, through sleepy eyelids. "You're worse than Pop." It was 4:30

a.m.

"You bet!" he said, as he threw up the blind exclaiming what a beautiful morning it was.

"Look at that sky—did you ever see such color? Smell the air—just think, some people have never seen how beautiful it is this time of morning—they sleep half their lives away, and so do you," he said, as he pulled me out of bed. "Come on, let's go for a fly!"

Going for a fly was not as simple as it sounded, for it could take twenty minutes or two hours. We had a hundred miles of fence and twenty-two windmills at that time, scattered from one end of the ranch to the other. They all had to be checked, as well as the cattle.

When we got up over the ranch, John kept yelling over his shoulder, commenting on all the beauty, the trees, the grass and the water. He'd point to a new-born calf or buck deer hiding in the bush or a coyote sneaking along the ridge. We'd fly over the prairie chickens' dancing ground and up over a hill coming unexpectedly upon a herd of antelope. If a cow needed help calving, we landed and helped her. If a windmill needed fixing, we landed and fixed it, and if a fence was down we fixed that, but if it was a morning when all was well—like this morning—we headed for home, buzzing the bunkhouse to wake the men for breakfast before we touched down on the runway.

As we taxied to the hangar, he chuckled, "In Pop's day that would have taken several days, but my day hasn't even started yet."

John loved nature and the Sandhills. He was happiest when he was galloping over these hills on his horse with his children chattering happily at his side.

He lived every day as if it was his last and had tremendous faith in God.

"I feel closer to God," he would say, "in these hills than anywhere else."

John always looked for the beauty in everything and the good in everyone. He wasted no time harping on other peoples' faults.

"Live and let live," he would say, and he did just that.

84

Chapter X:

The Love Goddess

It was a case of "many are called but few are chosen" when it came to finding a new girl for the house. When we did find one, she seldom lasted long. Late in the fall of 1957, I advertised for a girl and received only one reply. This was from a woman whom I shall call Tanya and who lived in a small town in northeastern Alberta. She wanted me to send her bus fare, but I needed help so badly I decided to drive the 200 miles to get her. I took little John along for company, and we drove part of the way through a blinding snowstorm.

When we arrived, I went right to the address she had given. The door was opened by a six-foot female of formidable proportions. Muscles rippled beneath her plain cotton housedress, bulged out in relief at the bottom of her short sleeves, and rippled on down the length of her arms to end in two great hammy hands. Ensconced in weather-beaten suede shoes, her large feet were planted firmly apart, her fleshy lips pursed in a thin straight line from one protruding cheekbone to another. Widely set green eyes glared through strands of canary yellow hair as she eyed me with open hostility. Thus might Horatius have stood as he barred the way to Rome.

"Waddar you wantink?" she rasped.

Abashed, I retreated a pace or two. "I'm looking for Tanya," I said faintly, hoping this was not her, but knowing in my heart that it was.

"Dat's me!" said this human fortress, confirming my mounting fears.

"I'm Mrs. Minor," I quavered. "You answered my ad.

I've come to take you to the ranch."

I was prepared for almost anything but the incredulous look which spread over her broad face. Her mouth hung open in surprise.

"Well, wadda yuh know about dat," she finally muttered, "wadda yuh know about dat."

Still apparently stunned by my words, she ushered us into the living room, explaining that she had been taking care of the old bachelor who owned this house. Then she left, saying she would go and pack.

"Deys come to get me!" we heard her bellow to someone in the kitchen. "Wadda yuh know about dat!"

I didn't learn the reason for her consternation until months later. When my family figured I had recovered sufficiently from my seven-day ordeal with Tanya, they told me how she had bragged to them: "I gots tree tousant dollars in da bank, and y'know how I got it? Peoples puts an at in da paper wantink a girl. I answer and tells 'em I come, but t'sent my fare. Dey sents my fare and I just keeps it and answers annuder. Dat's pretty goot, huh?"

In the meantime, little John and I waited impatiently, anxious to get started on the long trip home. Suddenly, our attention was drawn to two long shadows etched on the wall by the winter sun—undoubtedly those of Tanya and her bachelor friend, whose voice we had heard complaining bitterly about something ever since our arrival. As we watched, the two forms embraced passionately. Instead of exchanging amused glances, little John and I should have gotten out of there—fast. What we were really seeing was "the handwriting on the wall" as far as our peace of mind was concerned.

Tanya stayed pretty quiet until we got to Rosetown, Saskatchewan—about two-thirds of the way home. As we settled into a booth in a highway cafe there, her eyes fell on the juke box roster at the end of our table. She let out a cackle of delight. Retrieving a dime from the depths of her purse, she popped it into the slot, then sat back with a look of eager expectation.

Suddenly the song came on loudly. A female voice with a well-developed nasal twang was bellowing, "If You've Got The Money, Honey, I've Got The Time!"

Closing her eyes in rapturous delight, Tanya burst into a raucous echo of the song. Her body contorted awkwardly with the rhythm, and her face convulsed in an exaggerated dramatization of the lyrics. People at the other tables turned and stared. The stares became grins, and then outright laughter, as little John and I looked on in helpless embarrassment.

When, for final emphasis, Tanya lifted her bulk from the seat in ecstatic crescendo, little John slipped down out of sight in sheer mortification. He remained under the table for the rest of the meal.

But a worse ordeal awaited us at a ferry crossing south of Rosetown, where traffic had to be transported over the South Saskatchewan River. As I eased the car to a stop, Tanya peered fearfully at the river and then at the distant ferry inching its way across the current.

"Cheesus, Mrs. Minor, I'm scairt!" she yelled suddenly. "If I'd knowt we was goink on dat, I wouldn't uv come!"

"There's nothing to it," I soothed. "See, the thing is hitched to the bank at both ends."

But nothing I could say would calm her. "I'm scairt. Cheesus I'm scairt!" she howled, interspersing her outcries with prayers to the Lord to save her from the watery fate which loomed ahead.

When the ferry docked, I let the car run down the hill toward the landing. This was too much for Tanya. She slid to the floor, gripping my legs in an all-powerful clutch. "Cheesus, Mrs. Minor, I'm scairt!" she moaned. "It's da biggest boat I ever seen."

Anchored to the floor by Tanya's strong grip, it was now my turn to panic. What if this huge woman really was crazy? She might even be dangerous. The thought of what she might do to us if we aroused her wrath made me decide to humor her until we got home.

"What a nut," I heard little John mutter. I silenced him with a glance.

"See, we're almost across," I told Tanya soothingly. "Now that wasn't so bad, was it?"

When she felt the car's wheels hit solid dirt, our passenger surfaced like a monster rising from the deep. For the rest of the journey we drove through the fields of a neighboring rancher, passing line after line of survey markers topped with ribbons of brilliantly-colored plastic.

Tanya bounced up and down like a kid in front of a candy store. "I wanna stop and getta pretty bokay to put on the ay-reel!" she shouted.

I shook my head. "Those are survey markers," I told her. "It's against the law to pull them up."

I guess it was the wrong to say, for she abandoned her entreaties in favor of direct action. Our argument degenerated into a brawl, with me trying to fight her off and keep the car on the twisting narrow trail. Certain this crazy woman was going to strangle me at any moment, I pushed the accelerator to the floor. Every time we stopped to open a gate, Tanya would leap from the car in a frenzy of excitement, rush to the roadside and rip as many ribbons from their stakes as she could before I chased her back. By the time we reached the safety of home, I was sure I had a madwoman on my hands.

The men were playing table tennis in the diningroom when we arrived. Eagerly they filed into the kitchen to meet our new girl. I tried to think of some way to warn everybody that Tanya was unlike anyone we had ever had at the ranch, but could say nothing.

"What's the matter with you?" John asked.

Before anything else could be said, I was introducing Tanya to him, and steeling myself for any crazy eventuality. I was sure the woman would try to pull some shenanigans of one kind or another. But the introductions went off in the best Emily Post tradition. With only one introduction still to go, I began to think my fears were groundless.

This last person was Doug Cowan, a school teacher who boarded with us. As Doug's chief interests were artistic, he was an unlikely sort to find in a line-up of ranch hands. Maybe that is what attracted Tanya, for her eyes lit up at the sight of him. At the fateful moment, Doug's slim body was perched on the edge of the counter-top. Barging across the kitchen, Tanya grasped his finely-boned hand in her muscular clutch and pumped it vigorously.

"What's your name?"

"Doug," he replied.

"Duck, Duck," she cackled, "dat's a nice name!"

Doug grimaced with pain. Maybe she thought he was smiling at her for she suddenly seized him around the waist and lifted him lightly into the air. Beaming fondly, she whirled him around and around.

"Duck, Duck, I sure like dat name!" she repeated over and over.

"Hey, what's going on!" Doug yelled, as he flung out his arms and legs in a vain attempt to free himself. "Put me down!"

His feet moved back and forth with the speed of a practiced road runner, but to no avail. He was helpless in Tanya's clutches. There is no telling how long she would have continued to whirl him about, if she hadn't suddenly had a better idea.

"Duck, will you help me with my bags?" she asked, in a tone that was more of a command than a question.

"Sure," said Doug weakly. Still looking shaken and a little bewildered, he followed Tanya out the door.

The next thing we knew, Doug came tearing through the kitchen and on into the dining room. His face was ashen, as he paced nervously around the big table.

"Doug, what happened?" I asked.

"If I told you, you wouldn't believe it," he said breathlessly. Then he drew John aside and began talking to him in an agitated manner.

I longed to go over there and listen to what they were saying, but habit overruled. I sat in ladylike dignity, trying to appear disinterested.

Out of the corner of an eye, I could see Doug shuffling from one foot to another in embarrassment as he spoke to John in hushed tones. Occasionally he would laugh, but it seemed to be more of a nervous reaction than anything else. As soon as Doug had finished, John broke into loud laughter—the humorous kind which convulses the whole body. He laughed so hard I thought he was going to have a stroke.

When I got him alone later, I demanded that he share the joke with me.

"I'm not too sure but what the joke's on us," he laughed.

"Why, what happened?"

"Well," John chuckled, "as soon as that dame got Doug

out to the car, she grabbed him from behind. Then she growled into his ear, "Duck, you little bastard, sleep with me tonight!"

Tanya was an unrelenting seductress. She discarded her print housedress and turned herself into a drugstore cowgirl. When she appeared for her first breakfast, she was sporting a pair of high boots, tight bluejeans, a wide leather belt and a sheer white blouse with voluminous sleeves which were tightly gathered around her large bony wrists. The odd button missing from the front of the blouse was not of much significance because you could see just as well through the sheer material as through the gaps. And the inadequate efforts of her foundation garment to contain her ample mammary glands were calculated to boggle the mind of any cowpoke.

That morning John asked me to fly with him to look at some cows at Estuary, about fifty miles west on the South Saskatchewan River. Before I left, Tanya and I went over a list of things I wanted her to do that day. Whatever became of that list remains a mystery. When we got home we found that Tanya had attempted only one item—the preparation of supper. As a monument to her efforts a pot of cold, blackened potatoes graced the back burner of the stove.

But Tanya had not been idle—far from it. For one thing, she had spent part of the morning trying to pull the electrician off his ladder. In the afternoon, when a neighbor dropped in for a visit and decided to await John's return, Tanya had entertained him royally—as a sultan of ancient Persia might have been entertained, in fact. Instead of sitting down and talking to the visitor, she had jumped right onto his lap, wrapped her arms around his resisting head and directed his astonished face into her warm bosom.

Doug had an even more incredible (and terrifying) story to tell. As he paced the kitchen wringing his hands, he described a long series of indecent assaults.

"I tell you I'm worn out from running and dodging," he finished. "That woman's sex mad!"

"Aw come on, Doug," I said, "you're exaggerating. A woman would never do such things. Not in broad daylight anyway."

"Maybe an *ordinary* woman wouldn't," he admitted.

"But this is no ordinary woman!"

"Sure doesn't sound like it," John grinned.

Exaggerated though they appeared to be, these accounts of Tanya's active day convinced us she was not the kind of "girl" we were looking for. But John was preparing to leave at dawn for a few days work at the Kisby Ranch, so he had no time to dismiss her that night and I was afraid to.

"While you're away I'll gradually get her used to the idea of being dismissed," I told him. "I'll hint that there's just too much heavy work for a frail little thing like herself."

"Like an elephant is too frail to shell peas," John nodded.

"Well, I'll think of something," I promised.

Next morning, I repeatedly called Tanya to come and help prepare breakfast.

"I'm comink!" she would yell from her room above, but she never came. And that is how the whole day went. I would call, she would answer, and nothing would happen. My frustrations mounted.

Toward evening, I heard her thumping loudly down the stairs. When I arrived in the livingroom, she had just stepped back to admire two crepe paper cushion covers which she had placed at either end of the chesterfield.

"Ain't they nice, Greta?" she rasped, mimicking the men whom she had heard call me 'Gertie.' "They're for you."

My heart sank. In order to humor this wild woman I was going to have to endure the sight of those gawdy things in my livingroom until John returned.

"They're very nice, Tanya," I said resignedly. "Thank you."

With two giant steps, Tanya crossed the room and thundered back up the stairs. An hour later she pounded down again bearing a much larger paper cover. This she fitted carefully over the chesterfield, then once more stepped back to admire her handiwork.

"You like it, eh Greta!" she roared, clouting me soundly on the back.

As I limped out to the kitchen, I told myself that, if my husband did not return soon, I would go out of my mind.

Maybe it was the Scotch in me, but when I found that Tanya was selling ten-cent chocolate bars to my kids for twenty-five cents apiece I almost got mad enough to fire her on the spot. Not only was she making a handsome profit on the bars, she had assured herself of a steady supply of silver wrappers so she could create bouquets of oats and hay to decorate the house. I told the kids not to buy any more of her candy and prayed for John's return.

In the midst of it all, Doug kept embarrassing me by insisting that his chastity was in constant danger at Tanya's hands. Finally, I decided I had had enough of these inflated stories. Tanya may have been rough and tough, but I refused to believe she was the sex fiend Doug made her out to be.

"Look," I said, "so she has a crush on you. What's so awful about that? Some men might even be flattered. The least you can do is to humor her along until John gets back!"

"HUMOR HER ALONG!" he exploded. "Do you know what you're asking? It's like throwing a victim to the lions to keep them pacified."

"Come on, Doug," I scoffed. "Lay off it. You're just letting your imagination run wild."

"Okay," he said, "Okay! You don't believe me so I'll show you. You put on your coat and say you're going out to check with the crew in the bunkhouse, then you sneak around to the window and watch what that big ox does."

The children were in bed, and there were only the three of us downstairs, so I decided to humor him. Feeling kind of foolish, I put on my coat and came into the livingroom to announce my departure. Doug was sitting in an easy chair reading, and Tanya was on the chesterfield, half a length of the room away. After I had said my little piece, I pushed out into the snowy night.

By the time I arrived back at the window, the attack was well in progress. Tanya had launched herself at Doug the minute the door closed. He slid away down in the chair lifting his legs in a desperate effort to ward her off. While I stared in amazement, Doug was pumping his legs like an upside-down cyclist, shouting at his amorous attacker to go away. Meantime, Tanya was thrusting her long arms wildly at this legs trying to break through his defense. Her onslaught continued until I rushed back into the livingroom, at which she disappeared up to her room.

"Now do you believe me?" Doug panted.

I could only nod, for I was panting heavily, too. I had really burned up the snow rushing back in there to save him from a fate worse than death.

Night after night, we lived in an aura of tension. Clad in a flimsy nightgown, Tanya would hover patiently behind the crack of her slightly opened door, waiting for the sound of Doug mounting the stairs to bed. As he reached the top stair, Doug would see her mammoth form beckoning with a crooked index finger and would light out for his room in terror. Only the dexerity of his lithe body saved him on such occasions. Somehow he always managed to reach his door a split second ahead of his relentless pursuer. Slamming the door in her face, he would bolt it hurriedly and stand there panting while he recovered his breath. This nightly exercise kept Doug in tip top shape for the rest of the winter, but I wouldn't recommend it for anyone with a weak heart.

Like the wildcat she was, Tanya required very little sleep. Three or four hours completely rejuvenated her. This left her ample time to shuffle back and forth along the hallway, pausing at each bedroom door to check the breathing of the sleepers within. Sometimes she would patter down the stairs and out to the bunkhouse, where she amused herself by tossing snowballs at the windows. When Doug heard her on the move, he would clutch the baton he kept by his pillow, determined to sell himself dearly. The rest of us merely listened and trembled, catching what sleep we could until the long night watch could safely be abandoned.

To this tension-ridden household John returned late one evening. Innocent of our predicament, he had brought a neighbor to share the vaunted Minor hospitality.

Meanwhile, exhausted by his nights of vigil, Doug had carelessly dozed off, leaving his door unlatched. As the only extra bed was in Doug's room, John directed the neighbor in there to sleep. The minute the hapless man opened the door, Doug jerked awake. Seizing his baton, Doug hurled himself valiantly at the intruder. We heard the neighbor yell out in alarm.

John got to the door just as the lights went on. Then explosions of laughter rocked the house as Doug told John and our guest the reason for his actions.

"She goes first thing in the morning," John promised, still

chuckling over the sight of Doug standing there in his pajamas with the baton clutched desperately in his hands.

It was my fearsome duty to drive Tanya to the bus stop in Abbey. Certain that she would attack me at any moment, I drove with the accelerator pressed right to the floor, hoping that our breakneck pace would put her in such a state of fright she would have no time to think of going on the offensive. At last the familiar elevators came into view. Heart racing, I screeched the car to a halt in front of the bus stop, bounced out and tossed the sulky siren's bags up on the sidewalk. Then I went in and bought her a ticket.

"Goot bye, Greta," Tanya said darkly. "I guess the mens are yours now."

"Goodbye," I said hurriedly, too intent on escaping to ponder her words. Jumping into the car, I spun the tires and raced away, leaving her standing there in sullen majesty. Free at last, I exulted, happy in the knowledge that my suffering was over.

But it wasn't, as I found out later. In the short five-minute wait for her bus, Tanya had managed to create enough of a sensation to ensure that the local gossips would have a rich store of material to chew on for the rest of the winter. In booming tones, she had informed every soul in the waiting room that, "Greta wants all the mens out der for herself."

Chapter XI:

Many Hands Make Work

In those days, any job seeker who rode, walked, or even crawled to our gate was hired on the spot. A man's background (or even his foreground) was unimportant. If he looked as if he could do a day's work, John hired him. Even if he looked like he *couldn't* do a day's work, John felt sorry for him and hired him anyway. John did all his hiring at the gate. He never scouted around for men with ranching experience. Our gate was a sort of outdoor Manpower Center. As a result, we never knew what kind of people we had living in our bunkhouse.

One summer day, a fellow named Andy drove into our yard in a much-abused Model "A," and was soon unpacking his suitcase in the bunkhouse. For three whole days we marveled at our good fortune. Andy was clean, orderly, friendly, trustworthy and reliable. He was what we had always wanted. The trouble was that others wanted him too.

One Sunday Andy was busy shaving and the children were sitting on a nearby bunk admiring his dexterity with the straight razor. He had just shaved the lather off one side of his face, when suddenly the door flew open and two policemen charged in with drawn revolvers. They told him to put down the razor, and then they handcuffed him.

"Hey, what's the big idea?" Andy protested. "The least you could do is give a man a chance to finish shaving!"

"Where you're going it's very informal," one of the officers told him. "Just come the way you are."

With one side of his face still lathered, he was marched out the door to the waiting police car, leaving the other hands and the children to stare in wide-eyed wonder. After they had recovered from the shock, they named him "Andy Halfwhiskers."

Then there was the Sunday morning when John went out to waken the men and saw the worn soles of a very large pair of feet poking through the open window of our truck. Not recognizing the feet, he continued on to the bunkhouse, where he found the men recovering from their usual Saturday night in town.

"That fella in the truck a friend of any of you fellas?" he asked.

One by one, the crew denied any knowledge of him. Most of them couldn't remember picking up any strangers at all.

Later, when John was outside detailing some of the chores that had to be done, the rest of the body emerged from the truck. As soon as it had assumed a more-or-less upright position, it weaved its way over to John and a deep, mournful voice asked if there were any jobs available.

As a potential ranch hand, this man's appearance was anything but promising. He had a small, round face which wobbled uncertainly atop a thin neck. Long arms dangled down almost to the knees of his short, spindly legs. On his head was an oversized Boy Scout-style black Stetson, with a straight, flat brim that gave a brooding look to eyes of infinite sadness.

"This time you've really picked a dandy," I said. "How much work do you expect to get out of him?"

"He'll be all right," John told me. "Anyway, he looks like he needs a job."

Later, our new hand appeared at the kitchen door, and solemnly handed me an official-looking paper. "Woman, put this paper away in a safe place," he said in that funereal voice of his.

Glancing at it, I found that it was a release paper from a mental hospital. It stated that our new employee was quite harmless and once again fit to take his place in society. I watched the man as he trudged down the path toward the bunkhouse and told myself consolingly that he must be all right. After all, he was the only one at the Minor Ranch who could prove he wasn't crazy and that was something.

"Did you know about this?" I asked John, indicating the

paper.

He nodded uncomfortably. "Sure, he showed it to me. But I had to hire the poor guy. He looked so sad."

For the rest of the summer I worried about the man's presence on the ranch. From the look of him, and the way he sometimes acted, I had reason to question the validity of the statement on that paper. Knowing that our stranger did very little work, I encouraged John to let him go.

"Heck, somebody has to look after him," John said.

"Well, why does it have to be you?"

"I don't know. Guess I'm just lucky."

The man stayed with us until fall when John always laid off some of the crew. A person should be thankful for small mercies, I told myself. I would sure hate to be stuck with someone like that all winter. Before leaving, our friend appeared at my kitchen door again and asked for his paper in the same polite manner. "Woman, I want my paper." I heaved a sigh of relief as I retrieved his precious document from a vase on the plate railing.

"I'm sure glad that one is gone," I said to John at suppertime. "He worried me. I hope you won't hire him again."

But one Sunday morning next August, we looked toward the bunkhouse to see the same large feet protruding from the window of our truck.

I looked at John in alarm. "Surely you're not going to hire him again?"

"Nope," he said, as he headed toward the door, "I'm not going to hire him. I'll let him down easy."

Within minutes, I heard a knock at the door and opened it to find that familiar figure standing there with his written proof that he was the only sane one among us. By this time, I was beginning to believe it. The instructions had not changed one iota:

"Woman, put this paper away in a safe place."

When John returned, I was in a fine rage. But he just shrugged his shoulders and grinned. "The poor guy looked so mournful, I couldn't resist him. Heck, anybody can use a pitchfork."

"It's the way he might decide to use it that worries me!" I snapped.

On one of their Saturday night trips to town, the crew was told to bring back our three-ton truck, which had been in Abbey for repairs. At four o'clock next morning, John and I awoke to the sound of someone pounding frantically on the kitchen door.

He went down to find one of the men all covered with blood and in a great state of agitation. After he had calmed down a bit, the man told how the rest of the crew tried to murder him as they drove home in the truck.

"The only way I saved my life was by diving out the open window as we rolled along," he said. "I lay there for awhile with the wind knocked out of me, then I crawled home across the fields."

When the rest of the men failed to appear with the truck, John went up in the airplane to search for them. He located them in the middle of the Sandhills, then flew home to get a truck so he could go and get them.

Once home, each one gave his version of the fight, and all of them differed. Each claimed that he had merely been an onlooker, and that one of the others had started the trouble. But no one mentioned a fellow called "John Barleycorn" who had probably played a big hand in the events. Finally, John had had enough.

"The way I see it, one's as bad as the other," he said. "Seeing as I can't take anybody's word for what happened. you'll all have to go."

Included in this blanket dictum was the only certifiably sane man on the ranch. By nine a.m. of the eventful Sunday morning, the official paper had once again been removed from safekeeping, and was once more on its way out the gate.

"Now there's nobody to do the work," John laughed. But I smiled contentedly, convinced that you-know-who was out of my life for good.

But he wasn't. On a bright Sunday morning the following summer we again saw the now-familiar feet poking through the truck window.

"JOHN!" I said warningly, "if you hire him I'll clobber you."

"Don't you worry," he said emphatically, "I won't." With determination written all over his face he stomped out the door.

But the paper came in on schedule, as I somehow knew it would.

Within a week or two, this reliable fellow had run a steel bar through our new hammer mill, bending all the blades so that they had to be removed, straightened and replaced. This repair job took several days, smack in the middle of harvest when every moment counts.

"Don't expect any sympathy from me," I told John, crisply.

"I don't deserve any," he agreed. "Someone has to take care of this guy, but why should it always be me? A few more hands like that and we'd go broke for sure."

While John was trying to decide how he could let the man go without hurting his feelings, word came through that our friend had wet his bed. Flooded it, would have been a better word. He had created a pool which overflowed the edge and ran down into the occupied bunk below. The howl that came up would have done a timber wolf proud. Next morning, the official paper made its final journey down the road.

Several years later, a letter arrived from him asking if he could have his old job back. This time—he promised—he would be very good. He even included a touching little bit about his great desire to return to the land "where the deers and the antelopes play."

But without those sad eyes and mournful voice to haunt him, John was able to say no.

John and I had many a squabble over the type of man we should hire. A typical quarrel developed after the arrival of two teenagers, Richard and Donald, who had grown up together. Richard was fifteen and Donald eighteen. Both had already had some ranch experience, and they soon developed into top men.

By nature, the two were poles apart. While Don was effusively friendly, visiting with the family during most of his spare time, Richard was the quiet type who seldom spoke. At one minute past six every Saturday evening, Richard would leave the ranch, spinning the wheels of his old car as he raced out of the yard. Late Sunday night he would return, red-eyed and hollow-cheeked. All week he would shun

99

our polite living room discussions for the less civilized diversions of roping, riding and breaking horses.

Although he was good at his work, Richard seemed the epitome of the delinquent teenager, and I was worried about his effect on the children. Our youngest two, Barry and Susan, were always out in the corral with him. He was absolutely without fear, and the children admired this. I spent a good deal of time trying to change Richard, hoping that he would develop into a young gentleman like Don. But he was not the type you could easily mold.

"Aw leave him alone," said John, when I told him of my worries. "He's got a good head on his shoulders. You just wait—he's going to amount to something some day."

Don and Richard had been on the ranch five years when the latter really put his foot in it. One weekend, John told him to be sure and be back on Sunday to help move some cattle, and he promised he would. But Sunday afternoon rolled around and still no Richard. John was furious.

"I told you he was unreliable," I said, as we all went out to help with the herd.

Next morning, Richard came back in time to join the men as John was giving them their instructions for the day. When he came to Richard, John said firmly, "And you can go."

John came back into the kitchen and there were tears in his eyes. I was astonished, for it was the first time I had ever seen him that way.

"Don't feel so badly," I told him, "he'll be back."

"I can't help it," John said softly, "when you've had a guy around for five years you grow awfully fond of him."

In the next few years our calf crop began to decline alarmingly, and John was really worried. It's the same as a production line slowdown in a manufacturing plant, only more so, because you work on a smaller profit margin in the cattle business. John suspected a disease called Vibriosis (contagious abortion).

"Are you sure that's what it is?" I asked.

He shook his head. "The only thing I'm sure of is that we're not getting as many calves."

"Can't you have the cows tested to see if they have it?"

"That's a pretty tall order for a big herd like ours, especially when they're spread out all over the Sandhills."

At that time, the herd consisted of about 1,400 breeding cows, about 1,000 of them straight Herefords. The rest were crossbreds of Hereford-Angus and Hereford-Shorthorn blood.

"Well, there must be *something* you can do," I argued.

"There is," he told me, "mass artificial insemination. And I'm just crazy enough to try it. Some of the dairy fellows have used it on a smaller scale."

"Did it work?"

"Not very well," he admitted, "but the veterinarians and experimental farm people say it *will* work if it's done right."

"There's still the job of rounding up those cattle," I pointed out. "You can't just stand on a hill and blow a whistle."

For a moment John stood there, then his face broke into a broad grin. "Say, maybe you've got something! We can't blow a whistle, but we sure can blow a windmill!"

"What do you mean?"

"Those cows have to come to water, don't they?" he said, growing more enthusiastic as he talked. "Suppose we build corrals at each windmill. We're bound to catch every cow at least once a day!"

"You're right!" I cried, getting excited myself. Then I had a sobering afterthought. I had come a long way since those days when I wondered where calves came from, and I knew there was no use servicing a cow unless she was in heat.

"But how are you going to tell which ones are ready?"

"I'll find a way," John said stubbornly, and he did.

Our great experiment began about June 30, 1957. John's sister Alice and her husband, Rex Bovee, came over from Cabri to help us set up our insemination camps. And so we became the first large-scale ranching operation to use artificial insemination on a big herd of cows under range conditions.

Said Charles Koch, writing in the American magazine, "The Farm Quarterly": "John Minor comes of pioneer stock who pushed past the bones of those who didn't make it. He is not one to be discouraged by the failures of others."

How did our riders figure out which cows were in heat?

101

They didn't—they let the bulls do that. Fitted with a belt and apron so they couldn't breed, these "locator" bulls would march out to meet the incoming herd, looking for prospects. Our cowboys followed a discreet distance behind. Every cow the bulls "made advances to," our boys would gently nudge toward the improvised corrals, leaving the frustrated Romeos to continue their fruitless search.

Frozen semen had been flown in from Waterloo, Ontario, and stored in alcohol and dry ice in one of the cookhouses. Murrell Bowman, a young veterinary student from Guelph, Ontario, did the inseminating. And what a job he did—handling as many as 100 servicings some days! After forty-two days the big job was completed.

That summer the eyes of a good part of the cattle world were focused on the Minor Ranch. During the month of July alone, dozens of visitors registered in our guest book. They came by car and plane from all over North America. Some came from as far away as Australia and Venezuela, and letters poured in by the hundreds.

As Frank Jacobs of "Canadian Cattlemen" put it: "Some jeered, a few waited and watched—thankful it was John and not they that were doing it."

When we pregnancy tested in the fall, our conception rate was 85%, proving our artificial insemination program was a huge success.

Chapter XII:

A Mighty Big Spread!

Small things often herald the start of large events. In this case it was a long distance phone call from John.

"Where are you calling from?" I shouted, as I tried to make myself heard above the clamor of the kids.

"From B.C. Say honey, I've found just the place we've been looking for. The Chilco Ranch in the Cariboo country. There's a million acres here! Room for everybody. Jim Quigly can be a part of it too. It's so tremendous it will take a lot of management and a lot of help!" His voice vibrated with excitement. The year was 1961.

Jim Quigly was a young Nebraskan who was also looking for a ranch. He had worked for us during the summer with our A.I. program.

John had been thinking about leaving the Sandhills country for some time. Not by choice, but because the Saskatchewan government was reported to be considering a land lease policy whereby Crown leases would not be renewed when their terms expired. The Minor Ranch depended on the use of Crown land for a viable livestock operation. He enquired of the Minister of Agriculture, who confirmed that this was the intended policy.

"Then we will leave this province," John said. "Ranching is my life. It's all I know and all I care to know."

"I hope you won't do that," the Minister replied.

It was hard for John to imagine leaving a place his father had settled on in the late 1800's, building it up from the vast wilderness to its present state, but John wasn't a guy to sit around feeling sorry for himself.

So with this piece of legislation to spur his efforts, John

had joined Jim Quigly in his search for a new ranch as soon as the summer work was done.

Hearing the excitement in his voice now, as he told me about the Chilco, I knew that this was not just another Milley Place or Kisbey Ranch—one that we would eventually have to return home from. This time we would be leaving the Sandhills for good.

"You mean we'll move away out there?" I asked, my tone a mixture of anxiety and elation.

"Why not? You'll love it!"

"But what about this place?"

"We'll sell it if we have to," he said. "Say, wait until you see the Chilco—it's beautiful! Of course, the house isn't much. You'll probably want to build a new one. I'll be back home Monday and bring you out to see it."

I sat there in a daze for some moments after he had hung up. Then I walked slowly away from the phone, across the den, through the kitchen, along the hallway and up the stairs to our bedroom. Once there, I broke into an excited run. I flung open the attic door and raced up the steps, where I spent the rest of the afternoon sorting through old clothes and packing two trunks.

We were moving! A new challenge, I thought excitedly!

One week after, John and I were at Vancouver's Sea Island airport, boarding a private plane which belonged to Mr. John Wade, owner of the Chilco. As soon as we were airborne and began to cross the rugged Coast Range mountains, I decided I wasn't going to like this new ranch—a million acres or not. This was dangerous country—this land of jagged cloud-draped peaks, precipitous canyons and dark forests. Looking down on it, I shivered. This could never be home to someone who had lived all her life on the broad prairies.

Then the scene began to change as we flew farther into the interior. The mountain peaks became more rounded, their flanks bathed in warm sunshine. We left the dense timberline and moved over the rolling green hills of the famed Cariboo Plateau.

"Why, it's just like the Alberta foothills!" I exclaimed in surprise. I hadn't thought anything like this existed in mountainous B.C.

"Much the same kind of country," John nodded.

We soared over wide valleys and uncountable lakes, and everywhere the green carpet of the land was sprinkled with autumn gold. I loved everything I saw.

Then we began to drop down and down and I knew we were almost there. A valley appeared below that was unlike any I had seen before. It was cut off abruptly at the far end by a thousand-foot basalt cliff which dropped away to a wild river—the Chilcoltin, I was told later. But the most amazing thing about the valley was that it was completely surrounded by a white wood fence.

We descended toward the grassy airstrip, circling a cluster of white buildings which nestled into a hillside covered with pine and fir trees. There were enough buildings to make a village, and they were laid out neatly along a gravelled road and expertly landscaped with evergreens, flowers and thick green grass.

As we taxied to the hangar where Mr. Wade was waiting to greet us, we faced directly toward a building which dominated the whole comunity—the magnificent Chilco ranch house.

"You mean *that* will be our house!" I gasped. I turned to John accusingly. "Why you . . . you were just teasing me all the time!"

"I wanted to surprise you," he laughed. "Anyway, it's not ours yet. You may not even like it once you look around."

Like it—I loved it! All I wanted was to get the papers signed as soon as possible, but I said nothing more. John had glanced meaningfully toward our pilot, who worked for the Chilco's owner, and I gathered that he didn't want me to sound too eager. There was still a lot of dickering to be done.

John Wade was beside the plane as soon as it stopped. He was a big dark-haired Californian in his early fifties with the build of a football player.

"Well, what do you think of it, Mrs. Minor?" he asked, as we neared the house.

"Very nice," I told him.

Nice? It was unbelievable! I was a country wife about to enter a palace.

The house actually consisted of two gleaming white colonial structures—a large one on the left connected to a smaller replica a few feet to the right of the main building. Wide red brick stairs led up to massive wooden doors at the front of each house. The tall white pillars supporting upper balconies and the leaded bay windows below reminded me of pictures I had seen of the deep South. A red roof completed this picture of polished luxury.

My assumed nonchalance almost deserted me as I got a closer look at the front doors.

"How lovely they are!" I exclaimed, before my husband's elbow put the clamp back on my enthusiasm.

"Yes, they are nice, aren't they!" Mr. Wade beamed. "They're Australian walnut. In fact, all the woodwork in the house is Australian walnut, all brought in from Williams Lake by team and wagons.

In the center of each highly polished door a thick brass knocker shone like a golden star, and a fan of bright windows arched over the top of each doorway. Inset in each of the glass squares were small crystals which broke the sun's rays into a maze of colors.

"A mighty fine door," John nodded, in spite of himself.

Inside the main house, we found ourselves in a large central hall where a broad staircase curved gracefully up to the landing on the floor above. Its walnut handrail was intricately carved and gleamed from much polishing. French doors with leaded windows opened into a large living room on the left and a diningroom on the right. The upholstery of the furniture was royal blue, and below it were Persian rugs of royal blue and red. Around the rooms hung drapes of red and gold, and each had a fireplace of brick and native stone. Through swinging doors off the dining room, we passed into the smaller house which held the men's dining room, a large restaurant-like kitchen and living quarters for a cook and cook's helper above.

My head was in the clouds as I wandered serenely through these regal surroundings. Each time I paused in front of one of the fireplaces, Mr. Wade would pile on a few more logs until the fires crackled and roared. He had heard me remark how much I loved a fireplace and was determined to sell me on the idea of moving to the Chilco. He needn't have bothered. I had been willing to move in the moment I walked through the front door.

For some reason the Chilco's owner seemed to feel that I was the one who most needed convincing, and he was prepared to spend the whole day with me, unveiling the wonders of his million-acre estate. I suspected that John had set me up as a sort of strawman to win more bargaining time and possibly a better price. I could hear him saying, "I'd buy it in a minute, but I'll have a hard time talking my wife into leaving Saskatchewan."

The next stage of Mr. Wade's sales campaign was a tour of the ranch. I would have been willing to skip this part, but I could see he was rather enjoying the challenge of selling a "difficult" prospect and I didn't want to spoil his fun. John, who'd already been shown around, decided to stay and have another look at the buildings and equipment.

Leaving the house, we drove in a battered stationwagon past the ranch store, several smaller houses—all painted white—a school, and an overgrown graveyard. At the valley's edge, we began a 1600 foot ascent to the Bell Ranch, which was one of many properties making up the Chilco. Halfway up the steep grade, we met a loaded logging truck which crowded us so close to the cliff's edge we sent pebbles bounding off into space. But the Chilco's owner drove with skill and determination—screeching around sharp switchbacks, waving to Indians driving their wagons down to the ranch store for supplies—all the time keeping up a steady flow of conversation as he related some of the history of the Chilco.

"The first Europeans to live on the place were a big, humorous Irishman named Mike Minton and his partner, Pete Bergue. They homesteaded a piece of fertile benchland on the south side of the Chilcotin River in 1884, and probably didn't run more than twenty head of cattle. But those cattle formed the original Chilco herd.

"About 1896, they sold to an Englishman named Claude Wilson," Mr Wade continued, "who bought out their one and only neighbor, a fella from Toronto, named Davey Allen. The first thing Wilson did was to add a swamp meadow to the ranch to supplement his hay supply. Then, when he saw the Indians working on a twenty-mile ditch to bring water from Big Creek to their reserve, which was near the ranch, he decided to join them and get second rights to the water. And that's how we got irrigation on the Chilco. Without the big hay crops that water brought, the ranch would never have been able to support a large herd of cattle."

"Did Wilson start the first big herd?" I asked.

"Well, he built up to about 300 head, and he branded them with a big Circle C. That brand was registered in Barkerville at the going rate of fifty cents for life," Wade added, "which is a pretty good bargain any way you look at it."

"But what endeared Wilson most to the folks around here," he concluded, "was the social events he staged in his house. After that, the ranch became a sort of focal point for the whole area, and it still is today to some extent."

"When did you buy this place?" I queried.

"About fifteen years ago. It had four more owners before I came along and just about every owner had added more land. A Cornishman, Joe Trethewey—who took over from Wilson in 1909—increased the area to 23,000 acres and ran up to 1,000 head of Herefords and Galloways. He also increased the horse herd from 50 to over 400, brought 500 acres under irrigation and built a sawmill. Then he changed the Chilco brand to the T2, which is still in use."

"Is this a good place to live?" I asked.

"The best!" said the Chilco's owner, emphatically.

"Then why does it keep coming back on the market every few years? At home, many of the big ranches have stayed in the same family for two or three generations."

That question might have floored a lesser man, although I hadn't intended it to come out as sharply as it did. But I was beginning to wonder about all those owners. Maybe we would be biting off more than we could chew.

Mr. Wade fielded the query like a professional. "One or two tried to expand too fast and ran out of money," he told me. "Some just did not have the know-how to run a big ranch. Not everybody is as experienced in this game as you people are," he added.

To one who had been called a greenhorn for so long, those were very welcome and diplomatic words.

"That's true," I agreed.

"As a matter of fact, the man who bought out Trethewey

in 1922—an Englishman named Langton-Johnson—did stay only one year," Mr. Wade continued, "then he sold to a movie magnate from Australia named Cozen, or Cozen-Spencer, as he soon started calling himself. Spencer was a sharp businessman, and he built up the ranch store business with the slogan, 'Everything from a needle to a wagon.' But Spencer's tenure ended in tragedy about eight years later. He was a mysterious sort of character to the people around here. One day there was a bit of gunplay and a killing. I guess folks were pretty jumpy for awhile after that."

We had stopped on top of a steep rise. My guide proceeded to point out some of the ranch's far boundaries and explain how different sections of the property contributed to the whole operation. I'm afraid I didn't pay too much attention. I was still wondering what tragedy had occurred during Cozen-Spencer's time. Finally, I could contain my curiosity no longer.

"Well, what happened?" I cried. "To Spencer, I mean."

"Nobody knows the full story," he said, settling back in his stationwagon, but I'll tell you what I can."

It seems that one dull, cloudy morning in September, 1930, Spencer asked his foreman, Stoddart, and his storekeeper, Smith, to accompany him to Deer Creek Ranch. "I think I'll take my shotgun along in case we see any birds," he told them.

The business at the Deer Creek property finished, Spencer and his foreman were standing near the truck waiting for Smith to lock up. Suddenly, the rancher raised his shotgun and shot Smith squarely in the back, just as the hapless man was turning the key in the lock. Swinging the gun around at Stoddart, Spencer fired again, hitting him in the arm. The impact of the bullet sent the foreman spinning and his assailant ran off, carrying the gun with him.

Recovering quickly, Stoddart made a tourniquet from a piece of cloth in the truck and bound his arm tightly to stop the bleeding. Then he went over to Smith. He arrived just in time to listen while the man dictated his last will and testament, and held him up with his good arm while Smith signed it. This done, he tried to make Smith more comfortable, but the latter gave a final gasp and died. By this time, Stoddart's wound began to take its toll. Feeling weak and

109

dizzy, he staggered to the truck and started for the home ranch for help. But his dizziness and the pain in his arm interfered with his driving. At a sharp turn, the truck veered off the road and rolled into the ditch.

Fearing the killer might return and finish him off, the foreman dragged himself from the truck and hid in a wooded area above the road. After what seemed like hours of waiting, he saw another of the ranch's vehicles approaching and managed to flag it down. It contained Mrs. Spencer and the ranch carpenter, Christopher Vick, who had become worried at their long absence and had come searching for them.

That night, a young policeman—summoned from Williams Lake—and the newly-appointed coroner, Rene Hance, traveled to Deer Creek to get Smith's body. A dismal rain had begun to fall, making the road slippery and treacherous. On arrival, they shone their car lights on Smith's wet body and noted the pool of diluted blood beside it.

"How do we know that Spencer isn't lurking out there in the darkness ready to take a shot at us?" said Hance.

"We don't," the policeman told him. "Well, you're the coroner, what do you want to do?"

"Right now I want to resign," Hance smiled grimly, "but we can't always do what we want, so let's take the body and get out of here."

With the dangerous Spencer still on the loose, an aura of fear and suspense settled over the countryside. Armed with rifles, the men of the Chilco Ranch posted a twenty-four hour watch. They had orders to shoot their employer if he approached. At the nearby Stone Reserve, the Indians locked the doors of their houses and went into hiding among the trees and haystacks. Convinced that her husband must be dead, Mrs. Spencer posted a $500 reward for the recovery of his body, and doubled it regularly as the weeks passed with no word of his fate.

Three months later, an Indian named Little Charlie was walking along the banks of the Chilcotin River when he saw a hand sticking out from a pile of brush on a sandbar. Investigating, he found that the hand was attached to the body of the missing ranch owner. Little Charlie collected $2,000 in reward money, but, unsatisfied with a job half done, he went back and scoured the discovery site until he found Spencer's shotgun, for which he received another $100.

When Mr. Wade had finished his narrative, we started back toward the home ranch.

"Did Spencer's widow hang on to the place very long after that?" I asked curiously. It seemed a lot of responsibility for a woman way out here in the wilderness.

"Until about 1938," he nodded. "As a matter of fact, she married the carpenter, Chris Vick, and they ran it together. Vick used the opportunity to build the house of his dreams. The house of everybody's dreams—including yours—if you buy it," he added with a grin.

"Mr. Wade, you're a relentless salesman," I laughed. "How many more owners did the ranch have before you came along?"

"Just the Mayfield brothers from Oregon. George Mayfield held it only a short while, then sold to his brother, Frank. They held it eight years and then my partner Ben Jeffey and I took over. I bought Ben's share and added the Scallon, Bell and Cotton Ranches.

A magnificent place, I told myself as we drove along, and one that had seen the broken dreams of a lot of very able people—people with the energy and know-how to put in an irrigation system so as to increase the feed supply, build up the herd, acquire more land and erect a sawmill, a store and a fine set of buildings. Would John and I be able to do any better? If we bought—and I was sure we would—how long would we be able to hang on before some disaster overtook us?

By the time we reached the main ranch I was exhausted, mostly from my constant fears that we would go hurtling off one of the narrow, twisting roads and end up at the bottom of some precipitous canyon. Excusing myself I went upstairs to rest. Remembering how partial I was to fireplaces, supersalesman John Wade kept the fires blazing while I slept. I awoke with the perspiration just dripping from my body.

During the remainder of our three-day stay he kept piling on the fuel so I wouldn't forget the crackling lure of a log fire, or that the ranch was well-supplied with fireplaces and timber. Finally we went home so that I could cool off while John made arrangements to acquire the Chilco.

"It's a mighty big spread," John admitted, as we talked it over. "But we could swing it if we had a good partner."

"Do you have anybody in mind?"

"Bill Gilchrist," he nodded. "The trouble is he's in France right now looking at some Charolais cattle."

Bill Gilchrist operated a fine ranch in the Cypress Hills to the south of us. Like John, he came from an old ranching family and had grown up in the cattle business. I was enthusiastic about the idea. Bill and his wife, Helen, would make ideal partners.

John waited impatiently for Bill to return from France. When he finally did arrive and John flew him out to see the Chilco, Bill became as enthusiastic as my husband. Before returning to Saskatchewan, they put a down payment on the property and agreed to take over January 1, 1962.

Once home, John sold our ranch at Kisbey to raise capital. He arranged to move his cousin Dode and family to the Cotton Ranch on the Chilco and persuaded his brother-in-law, Rex Bovee (who had helped us with the artificial insemination) to manage the home place when we moved to British Columbia.

In the meantime, the Saskatchewan Minister of Agriculture phoned to say that the Cabinet had reversed their decision. Fathers would be able to transfer leases to their sons.

"It's too late," John told him. "I've already made a down payment and we're ready to move."

Chapter XIII:

Westward the Wagons!

Moving would be easy, we told ourselves. The Chilco house was already furnished so all we had to do was pack our personal things. We could handle it with our station wagon and one half-ton truck. Reassuring ourselves that this would be a very simple task, we relaxed and enjoyed the Christmas celebrations. In fact, we managed to play down the whole business of packing so well that I was psychologically unprepared when John jumped up from the breakfast table on Boxing Day and shouted, "If we're going to move, we might as well get started!"

Suddenly we were projected into chaos. John started throwing books out of the bookcase into a heap on the floor. Each of our four children ran to his bedroom to collect sentimental treasures that just could not be left behind.

"You can't take that!" I cried, as one of the boys trudged into the den laden with long-neglected toys. "There just won't be room for them."

He began to bellow in protest. As I stood there with my hands over my ears, the others trooped in and the pile on the floor grew and grew.

By nightfall, we had packed countless boxes and loaded them into vehicles. We planned to head westward at dawn. I could not believe I was saying goodbye to the Old Ranch forever, which goes to prove I could have made it big as a fortune teller.

Next morning, John waved goodbye and took off in his plane. He had some business to attend to in Vancouver, but intended to be at the Chilco to meet us when we arrived. Watching him soar into the winter sky, I thought of the long, weary miles we would have to traverse before we got there. The Trans Canada had not yet been completed through Rogers Pass, so we planned to go to Edmonton, then north to the Peace River country and down through Pine Pass to Prince George, B.C. From there it was only a short distance south to Williams Lake and the Chilcotin.

In the station wagon, I had left a small space on top of the load, thinking one of the children might want to lie down during the trip. But as we started to get into the vehicle, our two dogs—Queenie and Lottie—jumped in ahead of us and climbed up there. They refused to budge and just eyed us defiantly. No amount of prodding could dislodge them. Seeing their determination, the children pleaded with us to let their pets stay. Rather than take the whole load apart, we decided to give in, although we had really planned to ship the dogs to the Chilco later when we sent our saddle ponies.

Animals have a lot more sense than most of us give them credit for. Usually the dogs never bothered to climb into the car when they saw us leaving the yard. But this morning they had no intention of being left behind.

I was a bit nervous about setting out on a thousand-mile car trip in the middle of winter, but I was determined to show everybody I could do it. Our ranch wagon was only a few weeks old, so I nosed it cautiously down the road, also determined to drive the whole distance without putting so much as a dent on its shiny new body. Leading the way ahead was our half-ton truck, driven by a neighbor, Eggie Elkink.

Reaching the Trans Canada Highway near Maple Creek, we were joined by two vehicles from the Gilchrist Ranch. In a battered old car, and pulling a trailer, was Bill Gilchrist's sister, Mary, who was going to the Chilco to teach school. Behind her, came Bill's brother-in-law, Carson Doubts, and his wife, Jewel, in their ranch truck. Our westbound wagon train was now complete, and wagon boss, Eggie Elkink, proceeded to "move 'er out" at a brisk pace, regardless of driving conditions.

We had gone only a short way when a couple of the children decided they were sick, so I became involved in a game of merry-go-round beds. The dogs also decided it was safe to abandon their perches on top of the load and seek a more interesting spot, preferably the lap of the driver. As I rotated sick children and excited pets in and out of the various resting places, I prayed that one of the sick ones would recover sufficiently to be able to sit up before any more bed cases were announced.

Arriving in Calgary, we stopped at the first motel we came to and called a doctor who set about saving the lives of our homesick children. Stomachs settled, we all bedded down to sleep in nervous fits and starts until dawn. Once more we fell in line behind Eggie as we turned north towards Edmonton.

Going through that city, Mary and I had one common concern—not to get left behind at busy intersections. We stretched the law a little here as I crowded behind Eggie, and Mary came dangerously close behind me as we slipped through one intersection after another on the yellow light. At one red light, Mary was unable to stop in time. In desperation she pulled out around us and went sailing past, trailer, kids and all. But we kept our little caravan together.

The great loop to the north was tiring, but otherwise uneventful. The weather stayed clear and cold and even the pass through the mountains was well-plowed and sanded. But our luck ran out in Prince George. Again, it was our old nemesis, the stop sign.

At the bottom of a steep hill, Eggie dutifully halted as instructed. I stopped too, but Mary didn't. Down the hill she came like a runaway bobsled and crashed into the rear of my nice new station wagon, dashing my hopes of delivering it to the Chilco without a mark. John would just shrug it off with a laugh, I knew, but I was still "old Sharpe's daughter," to quote Pop Minor, and believed new things should be kept unblemished as long as possible. To add to our joy, it suddenly began to snow.

It was late when we pulled into a service station at Williams Lake. We would have to leave the highway here and head west to the Chilco. Any ordinary travelers with eight travel-sick children, two dogs and a heavy load of goods and chattels—who had journeyed through unknown, mountainous country in a howling snow storm—would have stopped for the night long before this hour. But we were

115

Elkink's Raiders—the original Dirty Dozen. Eggie had been commissioned to lead his little band to the Chilco and lead it he would, breaking all travel records along the way.

"How far to the Chilco Ranch?" he asked the garage man.

"About sixty-five miles," the man said, "and it ain't exactly a paved highway."

"Back where we come from," Eggie told him, "that's only a whoop and a holler. Tonight we'll all sleep in our new home," he said to us, with the enthusiasm of a true Raider captain.

The road that wasn't "exactly a paved highway" wasn't exactly a road either in those days. I don't know which were worse, the whoops or the hollers. All I can remember is going up and down, down and around, until I thought I would go crazy. Through the falling snow ahead gleamed Eggie's tail lights, a friendly beacon in a world of weird shapes and shadows.

After about fifteen miles, we crossed the Sheep Creek Bridge. Below us, the muddy turbulent Fraser River hissed by on its way to the sea. On and on we bored into the darkness. Suddenly the road began to climb steeply. Up and up we went through endless switchbacks and not one white post or guardrail to mark where the edge of the road dropped off into nothingness. Lumber trucks lunged at us from around sharp corners, bullying us over toward the edge of the road. With each succeeding switchback, my hands trembled more and more.

Gluing my weary eyes on Eggie's tail lights, I prayed that we would arrive safely. Higher and higher we climbed, and I grew more nervous with each passing truck. Finally Eggie stopped ahead of me and walked back to the station wagon.

He was doubled up with laughter as I rolled down the window so I could talk to him. "Where in hell is this damn ranch," he roared, "on top of a bloody mountain?"

Then he leaned against the car and laughed some more. I got out of the car and joined in the laughter for it did seem we would never quit going up.

We started off again and climbed even higher. Then we came to a real mean curve and Mary's smooth tires refused to grip the ice. Slowly her car slipped backwards toward the edge of the cliff, while we watched in helpless horror. To our immense relief, it became stuck in the snow and stopped, but one rear wheel of her trailer was partly over the edge.

Eggie and Carson got out of their vehicles to look the situation over. "I guess we'll just have to dig Mary out," Eggie chuckled, as he came back to report. "We sure do have the fun, don't we!"

"If there's nothing I can do to help, I might as well keep going," I told him wearily. "I'd like to get to the ranch so I can put these kids to bed."

"Might as well," he agreed. "We'll see you when we get there."

As I pulled out, Eggie and Carson were trying to dig under the tires of Mary's car. Later, I learned that a couple named Olaf and Louise Sater, who ranched at Tatla Lake, had come along and stopped to lend a hand. With this extra help, they were able to free Mary's car, but they had to leave the trailer behind, with its rear end jutting off into infinity.

Soon after leaving my stranded companions, I reached the top of the hill—Sheep Creek Hill, the natives called it. Here the road straightened just as suddenly as it had developed the bends at the bottom. This was more like it! I was used to roads like this. My spirits picked up. Then, as the dark miles passed in endless succession, they sagged again. I began to wonder if I were on the right road. The steadily falling snow whirling through the gleam of my headlights began to affect my eyes.

It was close to midnight, and my nerves were just about shattered. All at once we came to a sign which said "Lee's Corner." A dim light gleamed from a house nearby. Happy at finding this evidence of human habitation, I turned into the yard, and thus just missed the sign post which pointed the way to the Chilco.

I knocked, and a little woman answered the door.

"Can you tell me where the Chilco Ranch is?" I asked.

"Just where the sign says it is," she replied in a crisp English accent, "turn left and about three miles up the road!" And she shut the door abruptly.

We were on a real country road now, winding and dipping down through low, wooded hills. I could see their dark shapes beyond the headlights' glare. We crossed another river—a smaller one. I recognized it, and could have shouted with joy. It was the Chilcotin! As we climbed up to the benchland above the river, I could see the lights of the house.

When we arrived we found Charlie—the ranch storekeeper—bustling around in the kitchen, preparing a big galvanized pot of strong coffee. As we staggered in, he came through the swinging doors of the dining room with a big smile of welcome on his face. He was a handsome, robust man with slightly graying hair and a ruddy complexion. He had been expecting us. I found later that Eggie had asked the garage men in Williams Lake to phone through and say we were coming.

After his warm greeting, Charlie disappeared out of the house, leaving us to find our own beds. It was two a.m. before the rest of our caravan arrived, full of talk about their adventures on Sheep Creek Hill and of having to leave Mary's trailer behind. Finally, we got our bed arrangements sorted out and dropped off to sleep.

But not for long. At six a.m. the jarring notes of a gong rang through the house. That was the cook's bell summoning the men to breakfast. Fifteen minutes later, while we were still trying to find clothes to put on, the thing clanged again. Hungry as wolves, we dashed down to breakfast.

The cook was a slim elderly man of about seventy-five. He appeared suddenly out of the kitchen in a tall chef's hat, white coat and dark wrinkled pants. His feet were shod in sandals that were liberally sprinkled with flour. This kind and gentle man, whose name was Smitty, was responsible for feeding the nineteen-man crew, as well as us newcomers. Ordinarily, Smitty had a helper, but when we arrived he was doing the job by himself.

After breakfast, I went to see his kitchen. I had been so enthralled with the main house on my first visit that I had given the help's side only a cursory glance. Now I could see that this large room was a dark and dreary place—so institutional looking! Cupboards stretched all along one end, and the floor was covered with dark green linoleum. There were few modern conveniences. Smitty did his cooking on two large coal and wood stoves, so a good deal of space was taken up with stacked wood. Dishes and cutlery were kept in a long rack in the room's center, much like you see in the kitchens of prairie cafes. I returned to the luxurious side of the house determined to do something about the kitchen as soon as possible.

Later that morning, John arrived with Bill and Helen Gilchrist and the Wades. Seeing our cars, he ran into the house.

"How did you people get here so early?" he beamed.

"You know Eggie," I said. "Once he makes up his mind to go somewhere he just keeps moving."

Eggie tried to look modest as befitted the leader of a band of night raiders, but he was obviously pleased with our accomplishment.

Then John Wade introduced me to his wife. The Wades were not moving out of the house for another three weeks so we couldn't get settled right away. Our first job was to determine who would live where. It was like deciding who would play which end of the field in a ball game.

It was decided we would live in the main house and that Bill, Helen and their daughter, Penny, would move into one of the smaller homes for the time being, and start building a new one come spring. The other families were given smaller homes on the hill back of the main house. The place was like a small village so we had no trouble finding a home for everybody.

All the houses needed cleaning, so each family set to work. By nightfall, the places were clean enough to sleep in, but it was agreed that everyone would eat at the main house until they had a chance to fix up their own kitchens. This all had a familiar ring to me for I recalled the first weeks of my marriage and our struggles to set up the original Minor home so we could live in it.

The next few days were a chaos of half-unpacked trunks, of scrub pails and woodpiles and homesick children arguing about whose turn it was to have a dog sleeping at the foot of his or her bed—of ranch hands testing their new boss to see what they could get away with, and of newcomers trying to become familiar with the traditions of the Chilco.

One of these traditions was the ranch store. Charlie's one-room domain was a study in space economics. Like the western frontier store it resembled, it had about everything a person could want to buy. Stacked high along each wall were stocks of groceries, meat, lamps and lanterns, pack saddles, guns, shotgun shells, a wide variety of western shirts, hats and boots, sweaters, watches and a host of household gadgets. There were cans of oil and gasoline, horse collars, sweat pads, horseshoes, ropes and bridles hung in profusion from the ceiling.

In one corner blazed a pot-bellied wood stove, always surrounded by a group of Indians, who talked, chewed tobacco and spat on the floor. They were as much a part of the Chilco Ranch store as the walls and ceiling. Toward the back of the room, a couple of steps led up to Charlie's office where this amazing man kept track of every item in the building and of every person on the place.

For Charlie was much more than the Chilco storekeeper. He was the kingpin of the ranch—the man who kept the books for the whole operation. He kept track of all money spent and received, of the hours worked by each employee, of contracts and shipments and produce and profits.

Charlie was also our liaison with the local Indians, the store's best customers. One tribe that lived high in the mountains and bought their supplies in six-month lots, dealt exclusively at the ranch store. And it was Charlie's job to keep count of the "jawbone," or credit, extended to each customer.

In summer, when the Indians were hired to cut and stack hay, it was Charlie who made up the contracts and knew when they had been fulfilled. Knowing each of these people by name, he could tell John were to find a certain man who could do a certain job at a certain time.

When the Chilco ran short of meat, it was Charlie who set the date for butchering another steer. A butchering was an important local occasion, as we soon found out, for one was scheduled for a few days after our arrival. As soon as the animal was brought to the slaughter house, Indians began to appear out of nowhere and climb silently up onto the corral fence to watch the proceedings.

They were more interested in the by-products than in the performance, however. As soon as a piece of steer was discarded, an Indian would slip quickly off the fence and collect it. When the butchering was completed there was very little of the animal left. Intestines and other delicacies were whisked home to the reserve.

Charlie hung the meat in the walk-in cooler just off the main kitchen. Because the chopping block was located in the kitchen, he had to come to the house and take the carcass out of the cooler whenever any of his customers ordered some meat.

Most of the nineteen ranch hands were Indians. In all our years in the Great Sand Hills country we had never had any dealings with Canada's native people because there were no reserves in that area. Our first meeting with these big, fine-looking men was more of a confrontation—much like Columbus must have experienced when he landed in the New World. During those first days, they looked at their new bosses with suspicion and we stared back suspiciously at them.

John and Bill soon discovered that these men were organized on a much different basis than our ranch hands had been in Saskatchewan. The Chilco hands were all specialists, and each one clung to his specialty as resolutely as any unionized factory worker.

"You go chop wood," said John one morning, turning to an Indian at his side.

The man shook his head. "Me no chop wood, me cowboy," he said firmly.

Surprised, John gave him a hard look and said what he would have said to any insolent hand on the Minor Ranch. "You chop wood, or you go up the road!"

The Indian stalked away up the road with great dignity.

Within a few weeks, none of the original crew were left, except for the cow crew—three or four men who rode with the herd and camped wherever the cows were grazing.

"This reminds me of the time we had to let the whole crew go back home," John grinned. "But hell, you can't run an outfit properly with men who will only work when their particular jobs need doing."

I remembered that other time well, and the central figure of that episode.

Reading my thoughts, John assumed the sorrowful mien of the "only man on the ranch who could prove his sanity."

"Woman," he said mournfully, "put this paper away in a safe place!"

"*You* will be needing a paper like that if you try to run a big place like this with no help," I told him. "Maybe you should try to work out some kind of compromise."

Chapter XIV:

Chores and Choreboys

On the third of January it started to snow—not the hard, wind-whipped snow of Saskatchewan, but great, soft flakes which dropped straight down out of a dark, dark sky. When it finally stopped, our valley lay under a three-foot blanket of down. Tufts of snow stood high on the top of each fence picket, impaled there like marshmallows on a stick. It lay motionless on the wires like a picture postcard scene, peaceful and serene. It filled the valley and choked the roads, and bedlam reigned on the Chilco.

With our years on the Abbey Ranch in Saskatchewan, we were sure we had tackled just about every problem you could meet in the cattle business, but this snowfall caught us unprepared. After our first few days in British Columbia, our heads were spinning with new responsibilities, new methods of operation, a new crew, and a whole new way of life. Three feet of snow complicated our problems beyond all prediction. Someone said it was the worst they had seen in sixty years. It always is, I thought cynically.

With the roads blocked, the men at our cow camp soon ran out of supplies. John was busy for the next few weeks flying out and dropping food parcels to them and checking the herd. The animals couldn't get any grass and it was impossible to bring in hay.

"There's not a single piece of snow removal equipment on this place!" John stormed.

"B.C. is supposed to be a paradise," I told him. "Who ever heard of snow removal equipment in paradise?"

Finally, Bill Gilchrist bought a machine to open the roads, but it didn't solve all our problems.

After the snowstorm, we tackled the job of getting our school opened up. It had been closed for many years and had to be cleaned and patched before it was fit for use. At last, all was ready. The children were primed, the School Board had approved, the inspector had inspected, and the pot-bellied wood stove was ready to embark on its precarious career as an oil burner. As John and Bill tinkered with it, I remembered our first oil burner and how Pop had fought against it.

How Pop would have liked this place! And I was confident that we could be just as successful building a place of our own as we had been in expanding Pop's ranch.

One evening after the roads were opened, I asked if I could go to town for the mail. John agreed with a grin. Our "town" was Hanceville, just across the Chilcotin River. I had never been there and I thought it would be a good idea to look the place over. It would be a change from the ranch. Oh, I had heard that Hanceville was a small place, but I didn't mind that. I had been raised in a small town. Coming into Abbey, Saskatchewan at dusk you saw only a single-lighted main street lined with stores of various shapes and sizes. There were a couple of filling stations, a post office, some churches, a few dim residential streets, the shadowy line of grain elevators and the dark plains stretching beyond. I expected Hanceville would look much the same.

It was already dark when the children and I started off in the station wagon. Banks of snow were piled high on each side of the road. Eventually our headlights picked up a sign that said "Hanceville." An arrow on the sign pointed off into the darkness to where a narrow track left the main road. I knew the town was close to the road, but I couldn't see any lights. Perhaps it is hidden behind a hill and I'll come on it suddenly, I told myself. That's the way things are in B.C.

As I inched the car cautiously along the track, I suddenly found that I had reached a dead end.

"I see a light!" cried young John, pointing.

Then we all caught a glimpse of it. It appeared to be a flashlight bobbing along toward us through the night. There was a man on the end of it who turned out to be Mr. Hance—postmaster, storekeeper, innkeeper and rancher, who, with his brother, managed the store and cluster of tourist cabins which formed Hanceville.

"I'll open the post office for you," he said cheerfully.

We all got out of the car and followed the flashlight to a nearby log cabin. Inside, Mr. Hance lit a coal oil lamp. Then he went behind a small wicket where the mail was sorted. We had driven right into the middle of "town" without knowing it.

There were many things about our new life that were going to take a lot of getting used to. At the ranch, our day began at four a.m. with a loud bang just under our bedroom window. This was followed by a rumbling noise, like distant thunder. At first, we thought something must have fallen over—like a mountain, for instance—but when it happened the second morning right on schedule we decided to investigate. It turned out it was only the choreboy arriving to start a fire in the furnace. On the Chilco, all heating and cooking was by wood fire, much as it must have been at the Dawn of Man, except that here we used matches instead of rubbing sticks together. This meant that every furnace-heated building had to have a wood chute—a tin-lined wood chute, in our case.

Working under contract, Indians chopped down trees and cut them up into the lengths we needed which they stacked in the bush. It was the choreboy's job to bring the wood in to the ranch, chop it into manageable pieces and deliver it to each of the buildings: the store, our foreman's house, the garage, bunkhouse, the kitchen range and the stove in the men's dining room. In addition, he had to keep a fire going in the furnace of the main house. He used full sized logs for this, about five feet in length, so that when he stoked the fire at night it lasted until he arrived at four a.m. the next day.

The bang came when he threw back the wood chute cover with vigorous abandon; the rumble started when he gaily rode the load down to land with a thud at the bottom. He always entered the basement by way of the wood chute. Whenever I was in the basement washing clothes, his Santa-like arrival always threw me into a panic. Standing with my back to the chute, I would jump in fright at the sudden thump of the cover above and then dive wildly out of the way as our grinning choreboy came sailing down over the logs.

"Hello, Mrs. Minor!" he would sing out, no matter how many times he had met me earlier in the day. Finally, John had to tell him to go through the kitchen and walk down the stairs.

The choreboy also supplied the huge wood stove in the kitchen. He would march in grinning happily with a big armful of wood held at shoulder height. Walking to the center of the kitchen, he would stop and let the wood drop with a crash. He never bent over so he could set it down carefully. That would be out of character and just about everybody in the Cariboo would rather die than be out of character. When he left the kitchen—still smiling—there would be wood and snow sprayed all over the middle of the floor.

Chaos seemed to follow our choreboy wherever he went, and his daily disasters always occurred on schedule. One always happened toward the end of each day as he was hauling in wood. He used to haul with a horse pulling a crude wooden sleigh. While he was in one of the buildings delivering an armload, someone or something would scare his horse. First, we would hear the rattling harness of a horse on the run, then a wild shout from the choreboy as he pursued his four-footed friend across the yard and finally the crash as the horse vaulted the picket fence and tried to take the stoneboat with him.

Somedays, just for variety, the horse would head for the barn. Often he made it all the way inside with the badly-damaged stoneboat still attached. Every day, about supper time, we heard the same rattle, shout and crash, so that we knew what was happening without having to look. And every day the choreboy would mend his harness, fix the fence and, if necessary, the stoneboat too. But it never occurred to him to tie the horse while he was delivering wood. He probably looked forward to this daily drama and wouldn't have missed it for the world.

Toward the end of January of that first year at Chilco the old cook left and we were unable to find a replacement for him. With no cook and no cook's helper, Helen Gilchrist and I took over kitchen duty. One thing we had really liked about moving to the Chilco was that we would supposedly never have to cook for a crew of ranch hands again. But ranching isn't like that. The only way you can be a gentleman rancher is to be an absentee owner and live somewhere else.

Helen and I spent the first few days scouring that large kitchen from ceiling to floor. We cleaned out several generations of cockroaches and removed what must have been a half century's accumulation of grease from the canopy over the cookstove.

For me, working in that kitchen was like stepping back in time about fifty years. At home in Saskatchewan, I had had an automatic washer and dryer, a dishwasher, electric wall oven, surface burners, mixmaster and central heating. Now I had to contend with a wood-burning cookstove and wood fires for heating. It was about as up-to-date as burning buffalo chips on the Prairies. I was cold all the time I wasn't actually cooking. And when I was cooking I just burned with frustration.

After being used to an automatic oven, I generally forgot to return to the kitchen in time to stoke up the fire. When I did remember, I would come charging from the upstairs bedroom, down those beautiful winding stairs, through the men's dining room and into the big kitchen, puffing like a one-cylinder pump engine. Too often, I found that the stove was cold and the dinner roast was as raw as the day it was hacked off the carcass.

John was still busy arranging for finances to wrap up the Chilco deal, so he was away a lot. It was while he was on one of these trips that the milk cows got into the grain and had themselves a rare feast. Two or three of them died before Charlie, the storekeeper, was able to come to the rescue. Charlie nursed the rest of the culprits back to health and another crisis passed into history.

But hard on its heels came a new one—the Gilchrists decided to move back to Saskatchewan. Bill had been unable to sell his ranch at Maple Creek to raise his share of the capital. For John, this meant finding a new partner or selling out and returning to the home ranch at Abbey.

"What do you think, Gertie?" he asked, "Should we sell this outfit and go back home?"

I shook my head. "I'd hate to have to leave before we

even got started."

"Yes, I agree," he said, "but whatever you say. If you want to go back we will."

"Do you want to go back?" I asked.

"No, I love this place and the challenge that goes with it," he said.

"And so do I," I replied.

"Well, we'll have to get a new partner," he said, "or a group of partners. We'll keep 'er going!"

So John set out again, back to the big country to see if he could round up somebody who had both money and ranching experience.

This was the signal for our cows to start calving. Cows drop their calves when they are ready, never when it's convenient. With John somewhere on the lone prairie, the little ones began to dot the landscape like daisies in a meadow. Water lay everywhere and the cows were weak from a lack of proper feed during the long, hard winter. This meant that their calves were being born in puddles and freezing before they could get a suck of warm milk to sustain them. This time, I was the one who had to act as head midwife. The tradition at the Chilco seemed to be that weak calves should be left to die. But after all those cold springs at Abbey when we drove constantly around the calving fields looking for weak babies, I could not agree to this policy. Our four children came to the rescue, working constantly. They brought in cold, wet calves and put them in the basement or into a heated shed, feeding them milk, giving them their shots, then drying them off and returning them to their mothers.

When John phoned from Calgary one cold March night, we were all sitting around exhausted. At the sound of his voice, I began to cry.

"I just can't stand it any longer," I wailed. "I'm tired out. We can't do all the work ourselves. We have to have help. There's just nobody here I can rely on."

"Hold on," he said. "I'll find somebody."

The next day he phoned back to say he had located my sister, Doris and her husband, Tom Hanna. They were already in the B.C. interior with their two sons, Stewart and Cameron, looking for a ranch to buy and had agreed to help us with the spring work.

"They should be there in a couple of days," John added.

After I hung up the receiver, I sat and wept once more. This time with joy.

True to their word, Doris, Tom and the boys arrived within a few days. I could have wept again I was so happy to see them. Doris helped me with the cooking and took over the feeding of the calves. Stewart and Cameron helped their father calve out the rest of the cows. There was still plenty of work to do, but the operation began to look like a cattle ranch again.

With them, came a breath of the 20th century in the form of a new propane stove for the kitchen and an oil burner to heat the men's dining room.

"That's two less things we'll have to chuck wood into!" I chortled.

"You mean you still cook with wood?" Doris gasped.

"We've been cooking with it, heating with it and until a short while ago, waking up in the morning by it," I nodded grimly.

The propane stove was a long, black restaurant model, with a big, flat griddle and two gigantic ovens. Compared to my shiny chrome wall oven and counter burners back home, it was an ugly thing. But out here it looked beautiful. After it was installed, I would stand tenderly stroking its black surface until Doris threatened to have me committed.

"I think being away out here in the bush has made you a little wingy," she said.

"After struggling with a wood fire the past two weeks I could weep for joy," I mumbled. "It's so easy to cook now that we have propane."

Doris looked without enthusiasm at the long black grill with its hundred strips of sizzling bacon and cussed. "Now you're beginning to sound like one of those goofy TV ads," she told me.

Finally, we were able to hire a cook and a cook's helper. Oh happy day! We were so glad to get them we were willing to do almost anything to please them so they wouldn't up and leave us. We developed a sort of master-slave relationship, with the kitchen help cracking the whip and the rest of us jumping through the hoop obediently three times a day. The last thing we wanted to do was incur their wrath.

Every cook has some specialty. Our's was punctuality. Punctuality at meal times was an obsession with her. Every morning she would sound the bell at 5:45 a.m. and again at 6:00 a.m., and if something happened so that we didn't get out of bed until the second bell, she would lecture us on our tardiness.

Fearing her anger, we would all leap from our beds at the first tinkle. I would rush out into the hall and check all other family members to make sure no one overslept.

One morning I almost collided with Cameron as he charged from his room, pulling on his pants as he ran. "On this place you don't say 'good morning'," he shouted. "You say, 'which bell is it?'"

But we never dared to complain, even when her meals were awful. Regardless of what she set before us, we took turns going into the kitchen to compliment her on her work. One day we arrived at the dinner table to find only a few potatoes and a small bowl of chili con carne to feed the whole hungry crew.

Doris could contain herself no longer. "All this and heaven too," she said sarcastically.

Cook gave her a long, hard look, but Doris smiled back innocently and the moment of crisis passed. The last thing we wanted to do was get in that kitchen again.

The next day when Doris and I went out to the corral to feed the bulls we found that the ground was only partly frozen. There were big soft, moist spots where the frost was beginning to come out.

"A sure sign of spring," Doris said. "If we're ever going to find a place of our own we're going to have to get cracking."

Her words depressed me. I knew she and her family would have to leave eventually, but things had been going so well I had just put it out of my mind.

"I'll miss you," was all I said. If I had tried to tell her how much, I would have choked on the words.

The bulls were restless, edgy—rumbling in their throats and pacing up and down. One old critter just stood and looked at us in an ornery sort of way so we gave him a wide berth.

"Another sign of spring," Doris observed dryly.

On the other side of the corral some men were busy

feeding the cows. We could hear them laughing about something.

Suddenly one of them shouted: "LOOK OUT! THE BULL'S COMING!"

Doris and I had been looking the other way, absorbed in our conversation. When we heard that shout we just took off across the corral without even looking behind us. Up and over that fence we scrambled frantically, landing hard on the ground, expecting to hear a crash and a thud as the angry beast collided with the sturdy fence rails.

All we heard was a roar of laughter. The men were just about doubled up at the sight of our mad 200-yard dash to safety. The bull was back where we had first seen him and still staring balefully.

Red-faced, we headed for the house. In TV westerns you see the rancher's wife reigning over her domain and all the cowpokes doffing their hats and treating her with due respect, but it seldom works that way in real life.

Doris, Tom and the boys left about a week later. The blow of their departure was lightened somewhat by the arrival of John's Aunt Kathleen. If you're going to go into the cattle business about the best thing you can have is a bunch of hard-working relatives.

Aunt Kathleen was Dode Minor's mother. She had been living at the Cotton Ranch—one of the Chilco properties— with Dode and his wife since last October. Being a pioneer woman in her own right, Aunt Kathleen could take just about anything in her stride, even wood fires. As soon as she arrived, she took it on herself to keep the stoves and fireplaces going. The job kept her on the hop most of the time.

"If I ever write a book about the Chilco," she said one day, "I'll call it 'The Log and I.'"

That was the closest I ever heard her come to making a complaint.

One morning I arose to find the house icy cold, in spite of the roaring fire that Aunt Kathleen had set in the living room. Wrapping up warmly, I headed downstairs to check the furnace. Sure enough, it was as cold as a frozen steer. Opening the door and peering inside, I saw only a large blackened log wedged tightly against the sides a couple of feet above the firebox. The only warm spot was the kitchen, and here I found the choreboy tucking cheerfully into a plate of bacon and eggs.

"Well, what happened?" I asked wearily.

"I sure had trouble getting that log in there last night, Mrs. Minor," he chuckled. "For awhile I didn't think I'd make it in, but I pounded at 'er with a big sledge hammer until she went in. When I went down this morning, though, I found the thing hadn't burned at all. I was so mad I tried to yank it out with my bare hands but she wouldn't budge an inch—no sir, not one inch!"

"The point is, what are you going to do about it?"

"After breakfast a bunch of guys are going down to help me pull it out," he grinned.

When the dishes were done, I went down to see what progress was being made. By this time, the men had left in disgust and the choreboy was standing there gazing at the unmovable log with a perplexed look on his face. Even his grin was gone.

"How am I going to light the fire if it won't come out?" he bleated.

I stormed over to the furnace, climbed halfway inside, and threw my whole 100 pounds into the fray, pulling, tugging, and heaving with all my might. Suddenly the thing gave, and log and I thudded out onto the floor.

The choreboy stared at me in amazement.

"The trouble with you is you don't get mad enough," I panted as I picked myself up.

He was still staring as I pounded triumphantly up the stairs.

Chapter XV:

The Moccasin Telegraph

My first personal contact with the local Indians came about two days after our big snow storm. There was a knock on the door and I opened it to find a tall Chilcotin standing there.

"My wife is sick," he said simply, but his eyes spoke volumes. He was worried and he wanted help. Further questioning revealed that his wife was having a miscarriage.

"Where is she?" I asked.

"It's that log cabin below the hill," John told me. "They have been staying there for the winter."

Helen Gilchrist and I followed the anxious husband through the three-foot snow to a little cabin nestled in the pines. The only sign that it was occupied was a thin column of smoke which rose from the small stack.

Hair matted and face contorted with pain, a young woman lay on one of the beds. At her shoulder and wrapped in nothing but a plastic tablecloth was a small baby of about three months.

After we had taken care of her the best we could, we went back to the house and telephoned the sisters at a nearby convent hospital and told them of the woman's plight. They said they would send one of the sisters. If the woman could be moved, they would bring her in to the hospital.

My next encounter with the local Indian population came in the middle of the following night.

Suddenly I awoke from a deep sleep to hear John's voice saying angrily: "What do you want?"

The light was on and John was sitting bolt upright in bed looking towards the bedroom door. I followed his gaze, and to my horror, there was a drunken Indian swaying dizzily from one side of the door frame to another! Sick with fear, I realized that the man must have walked all the way through the den and bathroom in order to get to our bedroom door.

John repeated his question, sliding out of bed as he did so.

"I want whiskey," the man muttered.

John spoke slowly, measuring each word: "You won't find any whiskey here. Now you get out, and don't you ever come into this house again."

My heart raced during that long moment while the intruder considered John's reply. Then slowly he turned and shuffled his way back through the house. Occasionally he stumbled and we could hear the thud of his body against the wall, or a crash as he overturned a chair.

John had his clothes on by this time. "I'll see that he gets out," he said.

"When you do, lock the door," I told him.

"Yeah, I guess we'll have to," he said reluctantly.

We had never locked our doors back home. It was a throwback to the pioneer days when a man's home was open to all who might be in sudden need of shelter.

One of the first things we learned about the native population was that the people always seemed to know what was going on at the ranch almost as soon as it happened. This, Charlie explained to us, was the "Moccasin Telegraph"— that strange mixture of intuition and word-of-mouth communication that kept the whole area informed about what was going on as effectively as a daily newspaper. "It costs nothing to produce and operate and is never tied up by a printer's strike," he grinned.

During our first weeks at the Chilco, we saw Indians fighting among themselves, Indians having a party under our bedroom window and Indians who appeared or disappeared without warning when you were least expecting them.

"They'll fight a lot among themselves," the former owner had told us, "but they'll leave you strictly alone." I only half believed him.

One day when John needed feed for the cows, he asked Charlie where he could get some. The storekeeper told him that a certain Indian could supply our needs and that the man could probably be found in the beer parlor at Alexis Creek. In the remote areas of the Cariboo, the local pub serves as an unofficial Manpower Center. In its own way, it is probably more efficient than the one run by the government.

When John and I pulled up in front of the Alexis Creek parlor we found a number of Indians standing around the door. As John got out of the car and walked towards them, it was obvious that they were expecting him. How the Moccasin Telegraph had gotten word to them so soon will always be a mystery to me. Somehow, someone must have told them we were running out of feed and would soon be looking for some.

One of them slapped John on the shoulder as he joined the group. When I first saw the man raise his hand, I was certain he was going to scalp my husband, but I relaxed when I saw no knife. It would be pretty hard to scalp anybody with your bare hands. As the men gathered around John, laughing and talking, I began to think that maybe Hollywood had overdone the wild Indian theme a little. Later, when an elderly Indian named Joe Atkins formed the habit of dropping into the kitchen to have coffee with me, I was sure of it, for we became good friends.

In Abbey, John had been used to running a small outfit and it was easy to keep track of his men. If something wasn't being done properly, he had time to do it himself. But he quickly discovered that running the Chilco was big business and that it was impossible to keep his finger on every phase of the operation at all times. He had to have men he could rely on. What John wanted was to build up a permanent crew of good men so he could delegate some of the responsibilities. The trouble was that good ranch hands were even harder to find here than in Saskatchewan. Workers drifted in and out of the Chilcotin like migratory birds, which of course they were.

"What we need," said John, "is to get in some self-propelled haying equipment. Then we won't have to have hardly any men at all."

When the equipment arrived, we found it created as many problems as it solved. Much time was lost moving the machines to far-flung hay meadows and, once there, they were difficult to service. Even a minor breakdown meant a major delay because parts had to be brought in from Williams Lake.

Finally, the lesson sunk in. If we were going to get the ranch work done on schedule we were going to have to forget about trying to impose our jim-dandy Saskatchewan methods on the Chilco and use the labor that was abundant and close at hand—Indian labor. And we were going to have to let them do things in their own way. This is what Charlie had been trying to tell us all along.

"You get in touch with the head man and contract all the haying," he explained. "They will move out to those meadows with their families and their horses and go to work in their own style."

And that's the way it was done. The families moved out to the meadows and set up camp, then they all worked together as a unit. In the fall, Charlie sent someone to measure the stacks so he could figure how much they had coming to them.

A few days before the start of the Williams Lake Rodeo, the Chilcotin Indians began their sixty-mile trek into town to attend the event. This was a big annual outing for them and they wouldn't miss it for the world. They traveled in horse-drawn wagons accompanied by numerous dogs that ran excitedly to and fro barking their heads off. The cavalcade stretched along the route like a page out of the last century while overhead the long vapor trails of big transcontinental jets ribboned the blue sky. Sometimes the travelers would stop and pitch their tents so they could fish or hunt. Then the delicious smell of meat cooking over open fires would come wafting on the breeze—a smell that somehow can never be duplicated indoors.

Several times during that summer we found our irrigation ditches mysteriously drying up. When John flew up to examine the head water gate near Big Creek, he found the gate had been completely closed so as to divert the flow onto the land of an old Indian who lived on the nearby reserve. John opened the gate and for awhile we got water, then suddenly it stopped again. This sort of thing went on for some time, until one day John and his men arrived at Big

Creek to find that the gate had been nailed shut with big spikes.

This time, John checked in Williams Lake to see just who *did* have legal right to this water. As he understood it, even if the Indian held first water rights, the old man wouldn't be allowed to block off *all* the water to the Chilco Ranch. To his surprise, he found that the Indian held no rights at all, so he went to the old fellow and explained the situation.

"You're welcome to use some of the water," John told him, "but you can't shut the gate. That's against the law!"

The old man just glowered at him. After John had left the village, the Indian gathered a bunch of his friends around him and drew a picture of John in the dirt, uttering cries of rage as he did so. Then he danced around the picture, chanting a song of doom that was supposed to put an evil spell on this intruder who would deny him the water that was his by birthright.

We heard of these dark doings through the Moccasin Telegraph and merely laughed it off as a bit of Indian hocus-pocus. But from that day on, the Indians of the district talked about the hex that had been put on John and wondered when the first misfortune would strike.

"It'll have to be a pretty hefty spell," John chuckled. "You know me—I'm the luckiest guy alive!"

And he was right. Things always seemed to work out for John. Maybe it's because he always believed they would.

Chapter XVI:

Two Kinds of Hex

Because it was the third largest ranch in North America, Chilco attracted many sightseers. The women, especially, were attracted to the house. Often we would look out to see dozens of strangers wandering through our yard. The bolder ones would walk right up to our windows and cup their hands to their faces so they could peer inside.

"Of all the nerve!" I exploded one day. "What do they think this is, a zoo?"

"Let's make faces at them," Susan suggested.

John was highly amused. "If we did that at their homes in the city they'd call the cops and have us hauled off to jail," he laughed.

Many relatives and friends from the Abbey district used to drop in to see us while they were holidaying in B.C. Still a little homesick, we were more than happy to see them. Entertaining was no problem at the Chilco. There was lots of room for everyone and lots to see and do. Every Saturday night there would be enough people around for us to have a dance in the living room. The ranch crew, our visitors, even the children took part.

We would bring down the juke box from the store, with its hundreds of selections, and dance to the latest Hit Parade pieces or the old familiar country and western songs.

But the dogs, Queenie and Lottie, were our one permanent link with our former life in Saskatchewan. They followed us around devotedly by day and slept by the children's beds at night.

One day while out hunting squirrels, Ross accidentally shot Queenie an inch from the heart. In a panic, the boys rushed the dog to the veterinarian in Williams Lake who gave her a dose of chloroform and then bound up her wounds.

"She'll live," he said cheerfully.

About two weeks later, Queenie tried to jump over a picket fence and ended up with a nasty gash in her side. Although we sewed up the wound promptly, it became infected and we had to give the dog daily penicillin shots. At night, her wound hurt so badly she had to sleep standing up so as not to put any undue pressure on it. Every time we gave her an injection, Queenie would begin to shiver all over and the children would start crying, thinking their pet was going to die. Gradually the symptoms waned until finally the infection disappeared.

It was about two months later that the children noticed a piece of wood sticking out of the dog's side. They pulled and out came a sizeable piece of the old picket fence.

It was after the start of Queenie's misfortunes that I began to have those dark misgivings again. Maybe it was the strangeness of this big country, but I seemed to have a feeling of uneasiness.

One day John flew home in a new plane he had bought. It was a four-seater, twin-engined "Comanche"—bigger and much more powerful than our old one.

"She'll do over two hundred," John said proudly. "I can make it back to the home ranch in two hours!"

"Maybe it's too powerful," I said uneasily. "The other was a good, safe plane and you were more used to handling it."

"It's the extra power that makes this one safer," he told me, "especially flying through all these mountains."

Then he launched into an enthusiastic account of the plans he and his partners had to make the Chilco into a real cattle producer.

As he talked, I just sat there—too lethargic to even look up.

Suddenly he stopped talking and said quietly, "When you're like this I feel like giving up this whole thing. What's the use if you're not happy. I'll sell out and go back to Abbey, or anything else if it would make you feel better."

I should have taken him up on it. Instead, I looked up and tried to smile. "I'm sorry, but I just feel down today. I don't know why, maybe it was all this trouble with Queenie........it will pass I guess."

John looked out the window to where Queenie was tearing around the yard after the boys.

"It doesn't seem to have affected Queenie," was all he said.

One summer night I dreamt that I was attending John's funeral. It was taking place in the church at Medicine Hat and I seemed to be floating somewhere above the large congregation that had gathered there—ranchers, cattle buyers and livestock officials for the most part. At the front of the church stood the casket surrounded by flowers and beyond that sat all the family. Beside our four children—little John, Barry, Ross and Susan—loomed a stocky, familiar figure. With a start, I saw that it was Pop. I called out to him loudly, but no sound came.

I awoke suddenly to find myself bathed in sweat. For some moments I just lay there, listening to the sound of John's steady breathing as the relief flooded over me. I didn't mention the dream to John.

A week later, the dream came back and I woke up sobbing. My crying wakened John and he held me tightly until I had calmed down enough to tell him about it.

"You don't have to worry about me, honey," he laughed. "I'm as healthy as a horse."

"Well, what if something *did* happen to you," I persisted. "What would I do?"

"Get married again," he told me. "You'd have lots of money and lots of suitors."

This time we both laughed, but the memory of those dreams left me with a vague uneasiness for days.

Toward the end of August, John began to complain that a mosquito bite on his hand was giving him a lot of trouble.

"I think it's infected," he said.

"Soak it in some peroxide or something," I told him. "The way you're carrying on you'd think you'd had your arm cut off."

"Well it hurts like the devil."

"Lots of mosquito bites ache a bit," I shrugged. "You don't have to worry until you see red streaks going up your arm."

140

At that, John gingerly rolled up his sleeve. To my horror, I saw that wide red streaks ran all the way from his hand to his shoulder. Suddenly I remembered my dreams and flew into a panic. Telling the children that we were going to Williams Lake, I bustled John out to the station wagon and set off at a mad clip.

"It'll help if we can manage to get there in one piece," he grinned, as I skidded wildly on some loose gravel at the far end of the bridge.

When we arrived at Williams Lake we rushed right to the hospital.

"My husband's got a mosquito bite," I began breathlessly to the nurse on duty at Emergency.

"A mosquito bite?" she barked. "Who hasn't."

"I think I've got blood poisoning," John smiled quietly, unbaring his arm.

"Oh my," she said, "that *does* look bad!"

In no time at all a doctor was looking at John's arm and giving instructions about draining the infection. We stayed in town that night and next morning the infection had begun to go down. When we told the doctor we wanted to head for home, he gave John's arm a second shot of penicillin and told us we could be on our way.

One day in late August, John sent Barry, Susan and their cousin, Trona Willniss, to move cattle in one of the flats. Barry was riding a bronc that had a bad habit of bucking and running off just when its rider was trying to mount. Otherwise, this was a well-trained horse and one of Barry's favorites.

We watched them mount up without any trouble so we stopped worrying. On his way up to one of the other ranches later that day, John flew over the trio just to make sure they were all right. As far as he could see everything was fine.

In the late afternoon I was working in the kitchen with Aunt Kathleen and Doris, who had come over from the Cottonwood Ranch for a visit, when we heard a great commotion outside. Then the door burst open and Susan and Trona rushed in. They were crying and talking at the same time.

"Quit blubbering and tell us what's the matter," Aunt Kathleen said sharply.

"It's Barry," Susan said. "He's been hurt!"

"Where is he?" I cried wildly. "Where is he?"

"He's lying in the pines up by the lake."

"Is he hurt badly?" Doris wanted to know.

"I think so," Trona nodded. "He can't move."

By this time, I was out the door and headed for the car with the others close on my heels.

"You mean you left him out there alone, unable to move?" I said. "What will he do if he's attacked by a cougar or a bear?"

The girls jumped into the front seat with me, while Aunt Kathleen and Doris piled into the rear. As we set out up the treacherous mountain road, the girls told us what had happened.

When their work was done, the three of them had decided to stop and swim at the lake before coming home. As Barry started to remount after their swim, his bronc bolted straight ahead, knocking him against a tree.

"Then he fell off," Susan said, "but his knee was badly hurt so he couldn't get up."

"Was he conscious?" Aunt Kathleen asked.

"Sure," Trona nodded. "He said that we better go home and get help, so that's what we did."

"We cut right down the side of the mountain instead of going around by the road," Susan told us.

But I could only think of Barry lying out there helpless. Maybe he would be attacked by a cougar or bear. Throwing my usual caution to the wind, I tore up the side of the mountain at top speed—around perilous bends, past rumbling logging trucks. "Barry could be eaten alive," I told myself, pressing my foot down harder and harder on the gas. "Why hadn't one of the girls stayed with him?"

In the back seat, Aunt Kathleen held her breath. Finally she couldn't keep still any longer.

"Gertie, if you don't take it easy there won't be enough of us left to do Barry any good!" she cried.

I relaxed a little after her blast, recalling that John had said much the same thing when I was rushing him to hospital in Williams Lake.

When we did get to Barry, we found him sitting in a patch of brush trying to keep his injured leg in a comfortable position. He was covered with blood from his scratches, but there were no wild animals waiting around to devour him as I had feared. Not far away his horse was grazing serenely, oblivious to all the trouble it had caused.

"I'll catch him and ride him home," Susan volunteered.

"No you won't," I snapped. "Just unsaddle him and let him go. He'll find his way home."

"If somebody held him and gave me a boost up into the saddle I could ride him myself," Barry grunted.

"You're going to get boosted into the car, and when we get home you're going to get boosted into bed."

Back at the house we were just pulling the last of the pine needles out of the cuts in Barry's back and bandaging up his injured knee when John walked in.

"What happened here?" he wanted to know.

When we told him, he lectured Barry about being careless around a horse that was known to be a bolter. After he had finished he turned to the girls.

"That took a lot of nerve riding down the mountain like that," he said approvingly, "but next time I think it would be a good idea to stick to the road."

"NEXT TIME?" I snorted. "As far as I'm concerned they can do all their riding down here in the valley where they'll be safe."

"Oh come on now, don't get excited. It's all in a days work, isn't it, Barry?" he said with a wink.

For some time I lay awake that night recalling all the ill-fortune that had visited us in recent weeks and I wondered if it were possible for an old man to bring bad luck to a person or a family by dancing around a crude drawing in the sand. Next morning I asked Charlie about it, half-fearful that I would be laughed at for my pains. But the storekeeper didn't laugh.

"A hex will work only if you think it will," was all he said.

In September, we rented a house in Williams Lake so the children could go to school. Little John was ready for high school now and we thought the others would benefit from associating with more youngsters of their own age, so the school at the ranch was closed. It was agreed that John would stay at the ranch and the rest of us would join him there on weekends.

Every Friday after school we made the sixty-eight mile trip home to the Chilco and every Sunday we drove back to town again. I became so familiar with the road I believed I could have driven it with my eyes shut, but John still worried about us. Each time we arrived home to find him in front of the living room window, restlessly pacing the floor. If we were late, he would hop into the plane and fly down the road to look for us.

The children made friends quickly in Williams Lake and began to participate in school life. In order to keep busy myself, I enrolled in an industrial first aid course. Graduation from this course would take a whole year off nurse's training should I ever find time to fulfill my old dream of becoming a nurse. This training could also prove valuable at the Chilco, I told myself grimly, if we went on having all these accidents.

The next one wasn't long in coming. This time, the victim was Tony Minor, John's second cousin, his official title being "cow boss."

One day while he was riding up at the cow camp, Tony was thrown from his horse and broke a leg. Two of the men brought him down the treacherous seventeen-mile descent to the Chilco buildings in a wagon. After this bumpy trip, Tony's leg was so badly swollen, his trousers had to be cut off so the leg could be set. We took him by car into Williams Lake where he remained in traction for a long time.

"Why didn't someone come and get me?" John complained, when he arrived home from moving a herd of bulls. "I could have flown Tony to the hospital and saved him a long, rough ride."

He got his chance to make a mercy flight a short while later when Earle Hansen, Tony's friend from Brooks, Alberta, fell off his bronc and got kicked in the head. This put Earle in hospital for several weeks with a skull fracture.

"At least they'll be company for each other," John grinned ruefully when he got home.

Now even John began to worry about his men. There seemed to be nothing he could do to halt the pile up of casualties.

"I shouldn't have just taken a first aid course—I

should've got my M.D." I told him.

While the children and I were in Williams Lake one week, the saddle ponies disappeared. They looked for them everywhere. John flew for over two hours but they couldn't be found.

As usual it was Charlie who solved our dilemma. With the help of the Moccasin Telegraph we offered a reward of forty dollars apiece for their return and Moccasin Telegraph didn't let us down. An hour later, the horses were in our corral and a couple of young bucks were up at the store to collect their reward. Instead of giving them the money, Charlie took it off the bills they owed at the store. The next weekend the incident was repeated. In annoyance John decided there would be no reward offered this time.

One day when Dode was riding, he found the missing ponies trapped in a nice enclosure with plenty of water and grass. He freed them and they went galloping home and never disappeared again.

When Joe appeared at the house for his usual visit and coffee the following week, I complained to him.

"Joe, why do your people do things like this?" I asked. "We are fair to them and help them whenever possible. Only yesterday I took an Indian into the hospital after a car accident to save him from bleeding to death. Why do they do these things?"

Joe looked at me for a few seconds before he said anything.

"Lady," he said, "some Indian bad, real bad, no good, lazy, can't trust, bad bugger and many Indian good, trust all time, work hard, good Indian. Same your people. Some good people, like you people, work hard, can trust, good people, but few bad, real bad, no good, can't trust. You see lady?"

"I understand what you mean, Joe," I said with a grin.

A few days later, someone came into the barn and attacked one of Susan's horses and then went out to the corral and beat up two others that were just being broken. When the poor animals were discovered by one of our men next morning, they had been bruised so badly almost all the hide was off their heads, faces and shoulders. Large, deep welts on their sides oozed with blood and matter.

145

"This is one type of 'hex' we can do something about," said John grimly, as he put a call through to the Mounted Police.

But it made me uneasy to know that someone in the district would do something like this. Our old Indian friend might incant the spirits to vent their wrath upon us, but this was something else again. Someone apparently had it in for us. And this was paleface work, because Indians love horses.

"What do you want the kids to do today?" I asked John as we were getting up the following Saturday.

"Nothing," he said abruptly. "Let's just keep them around the place here where they'll be safe."

I looked up in surprise. It sure wasn't like my husband to say a thing like that. But I said nothing. I was only too happy to go along with it.

Chapter XVII:

We've Got It Made!

Toward the end of October, John flew home to Abbey, to help work with the cattle there. After our hectic summer at the Chilco, he had been looking forward to seeing the Great Sandhills country that he loved so well. Compared to the Chilcotin uplands, there is nothing very great, or even hilly about this part of Saskatchewan. It is really just open grassland area, spotted with poplar bluffs, sage, ground cedar, brush and sand dunes. But it had been John's home for thirty-four years and the Chilco had never quite replaced it in his affections.

I watched as the powerful "Comanche" lifted off the runway and climbed toward the east, thinking what a wonderful thing it was that John could leave this remote valley and be there in just two hours. I didn't expect to hear from him for several days, but I was wrong. He phoned the first night.

"I guess it feels great to be home again," I said.

"It feels pretty lonesome," he told me. "This isn't home to me anymore, home is where your family is. I know that now. I can't get back to you fast enough."

"I never thought I'd hear you say that, John," I was almost weeping into the phone. "When do you think you'll be home?"

"Day after tomorrow. And say, Richard phoned me today to see if he could have a job at the Chilco. I'm bringing him back with me."

"Richard?"

"Sure, Richard Hughes. Our 'wild' teenager, remember? Only he's grown up into a real good man."

I didn't answer for a few moments and John thought we

had lost the connection. "Are you still there?" he asked.

"I'm here," I said. "And I think that's great news. We'll all be glad to see him."

The reason for my hesitation was that I felt a little uncomfortable at having to face Richard again after my efforts to have him banished from the outfit. My reasons seemed so petty now. What I had judged to be "wildness" was only a reflection of my own narrow upbringing. Perhaps the bigness of the Chilco and my encounters with all the different people here had helped me to grow up too.

As soon as I hung up the phone I told the children that Richard was coming back and they all cheered.

"At least we'll have one good man on this place anyway," Susan said.

And she was right. After some of the help we had had to work with in the past months, Richard would be a welcome change. I recalled with amusement my indignation when Richard used to quit work promptly at six o'clock every Saturday and not return until Monday morning, and then compared him with many men here who had never put in a full day's work in all the time they had been at the Chilco. What a treat to have a man who would work right up to six p.m.!

The only trouble was that by the time Richard arrived, my enthusiastic offspring had spread such rumors of his competence as a cowboy, the men became dead set against him. We soon saw it would be impossible for Richard to live in the bunkhouse with the crew feeling this way so we gave him a small house to himself.

With Richard, John's brother-in-law, Dave Willness, and Tony Minor, the nucleus of a trustworthy crew was beginning to form—men who could be left to carry out a job on their own and who would do the job well. Dave Willness, who was married to John's sister, Florence, took charge of all the irrigation. He had moved out with his family that summer and was living in a trailer at the Scallon Ranch which was near the Big Ditch—our most ambitious irrigation project, one that would irrigate thousands of acres of pasture land and eventually feed thousands of cattle.

The morning that John flew back with Richard, the gate at the Big Ditch broke suddenly, letting water flow into the ditch. Although the ditch had been partially completed, it hadn't yet been tested, so we didn't know if it would really hold water. But it did. As they flew over the site and saw everything was holding just fine, John and Dave let out a whoop and holler.

"At least there's something that works around here!" John said jubilantly.

From then on things began to run more smoothly at the Chilco. We didn't have a disaster for about a week.

Then, on the weekend, John and I were driving through our peaceful valley when we met Barry, who was on horseback and riding full tilt for home. There was blood and dirt smeared all over his face and he looked as if he was in considerable pain.

"What happened to you?" John yelled at his son.

"My horse fell," Barry said, reining up beside us. "My arm hurts."

"You drive home and I'll bring his horse in," John barked, jumping out of the car.

Once home, John hustled us to the plane and we flew into Williams Lake to have Barry's arm x-rayed.

"The bone is cracked," the doctor pronounced and he had Barry's arm put in a cast.

"I wonder what this hospital did for business before we arrived?" I said.

"You're good customers," the doctor agreed with a laugh.

When the children and I came home the next weekend, John suggested that we take the whole Saturday off. We all piled into the car and drove up to the Big Ditch just for the ride. That night at dinner, we turned on electric candles which were all around the room. Reflected in the highly-polished Australian walnut panelling of the walls, they added a touch of elegance to the scene. You could almost feel the aura of contentment which settled over the room.

"It looks like a feudal banquet hall," Susan said.

"This is the way it should be," her father nodded. "Maybe we spend too much time working instead of enjoying the things we have."

After supper, I conned the whole family into becoming my patients in an imaginary hospital consisting of the living room and entrance hall. I still had a long way to go on my industrial first aid course.

"I thought we'd had enough of hospitals," John groaned.

"This is a battlefield hospital and I'm a front line nurse," I told him.

My five wounded soldiers, little John (who was sixteen and no longer little), Barry, Ross, Susan and John, all played their parts with deep feeling, on condition that I would treat them so skillfully they would be well enough to spend the rest of the evening dancing, as we had planned.

Lying groaning on the floor, John suddenly stiffened every muscle in his body and began to shake all over.

"What's your trouble, Dad?" Susan asked.

"I'm dead," he said solemnly, "and rigor mortis has set in."

The others piled off their hospital beds to try some artificial respiration on him and the whole thing ended in a wrestling match.

"You're supposed to be patients," I protested.

"We've run out of patience," John hooted, "let's get on with the dance!"

And so the first aid stuff was put away and we got out our records. Watching John dancing with Susan and holding her as if she was the most precious thing in his life, I couldn't help remembering the day she was born and he had said, "Now my life is absolutely perfect." I smiled as I recalled her flying into the house when she was a little girl of four. She had watched her Dad assist a cow with a difficult birth.

"Mom, how are babies born?" she asked.

"Just like that cow had her calf," I replied nonchalantly.

"What!" she said, puckering up her face like she had just bitten into a lemon. "You mean to say you licked me off too?"

After our family dancing party broke up, John went into his office to do a little bookwork. The office was located on the main floor of the house, down the hall from our bedroom. It was John's favorite room. As well as the door leading into the main part of the house, it had an outside entrance so that his men could come in and see him at any time without having to walk through the house.

The room was finished in a light oak panelling. Filing

cabinets, shelves and a large veterinary supply cabinet occupied one wall, while a big oak desk and reclining office chair dominated the position in front of the window. The costly Persian rug on the floor was well worn from many years of use. With our addition of an easy chair and a small chesterfield, the office became the most frequently occupied room in the house.

John was poring over the ledgers when I tip-toed into the office. I walked up behind him and put my arms around him. He smiled as our cheeks met.

"Honey," he said enthusiastically, bringing his fist down on top of the desk with a bang, "we've got it made!"

"Is everything falling into place?" I asked.

"You bet!"

Beaming happily, I sank into the easy chair and John swivelled around so we could talk. He explained how our winter feed supplies were stored in key areas where they could easily be moved to the various herds in times of stress. And how the Big Ditch would increase our forage production next year so we could get more cows.

Sitting there looking back over past events, I realized that, in spite of all our trials and tribulations, these past months had been the happiest and most exciting period of my life. It had meant the realization of my fondest ambitions.

John and I spent over half an hour recalling our many experiences since moving to British Columbia. We could laugh at some of our bad moments now although they certainly hadn't seemed very funny at the time. I was glad that we had moved off the home place and built up this ranch in the Cariboo.

"Everybody likes to come to the Chilco," I said proudly. "They can see how the place is growing. I think even the local people like to see a family working together to build something fine."

We went into the living room and sank into the big chairs in front of the fireplace. Happiness is a roaring wood fire on a cool autumn night, I told myself, contentedly.

"You know," I said finally, "your Christmas present arrived the other day and I think it would be perfect for you to have right now during the cool fall weather. Why don't I go and get it? It seems a shame to have to wait until Christmas to give it to you."

"Sure, why don't you?" John laughed, "unless it's a bathing suit or something like that."

"Wouldn't you be surprised if it were!" I retorted.

I returned a moment later with a new Indian sweater I had ordered made to John's measurements.

"Say, that's wonderful, honey!" he cried, giving me a big hug. "It'll be great for flying in. I'll wear it tomorrow when I go to Vancouver."

He tried it on and it was a perfect fit. He beamed all over.

"You know, I feel so good about everything tonight I think I'll go out and round up a few of the men and invite them into our rumpus room for a few hands of poker. They've all worked just as hard as we have to get this place going and they deserve a little relaxation!"

A few hands of poker, I thought to myself resignedly. Here we go for another all-night session. But that's John. He always has to transmit his enthusiasm into action. Soon I heard footsteps thundering down the stairs into the basement. I went to bed, content that we had all had such a happy day. Long after midnight I awoke to peels of laughter coming up from the basement. I smiled to myself and rolled over. Everything seemed to be falling into place at last.

Chapter XVIII:

I Won't Be Gone Long

The following day, November 18th, [1962]—began with the usual hustle and bustle as John prepared to fly to Vancouver. He planned to pick up two of his new partners, Bryce Stringam and Neil Harvie, and also Don Clark, the lawyer for our company, who were all coming out to the ranch for the day to consult with him about an irrigation system.

"While Don's here I guess I had better get him to bring my will up to date," John said, recalling a conversation we had had one morning.

"I wish you didn't have to go out there today," I told him. For some reason I felt uneasy about this trip. But when I tried to analyze this fear, I realized that I always felt uneasy about every trip.

"But honey, it's only out to Vancouver," John pointed out. "You fly west to the nearest ocean, turn left, and there you are."

"Why couldn't these people drive up here? Why do you have to fly there and pick them up?"

"Honey, these fellows are very busy men, and I don't want to take up too much of their time. This was the only day they could all come. Don't worry, I won't be gone long. We will all be back here in time for dinner."

"Well, if you've got to go I guess you've got to go. It's just that the kids and I have been away all week and now that we're here, you have to go."

"Look," said John. "Why don't you fly there with me this morning? Then I'll stay over in town tonight when I take them back and we can do some shopping tomorrow and we can come home right after that."

I shook my head. "No, I've got too many things to do right now," I said. "Maybe we can go to Vancouver for a few days holiday later on."

"I guess you're right," John nodded, disappointed, "but I'd sure like to have somebody with me today. How about waking Susan up and seeing if she wants to go?"

"Her clothes are all in Williams Lake," I said. "She can't very well go in jeans."

"Too bad," John said. "It would have been nice if she could have come along."

While we were talking, I was following John around the house as he got ready to leave. The kids were still in bed because it was Sunday morning and John didn't have any work planned for them. I just couldn't seem to settle down.

That troubled, uneasy feeling came again as I watched John slip his new Indian sweater over his head. When he had put it on, he moved toward the door. But before he opened it to go out, he stopped and turned to look at me. I was standing about three yards away in the doorway of the diningroom, looking rather forlorn, I guess.

When John left to fly anywhere I would generally kiss him and say, "I love you. Please be careful," and he would answer, "Honey, I'll just fly low and slow" and then we would both laugh. Today, he just stood by the door and I stayed where I was. All I knew was that I did not want him to go. A strange, almost puzzled, look passed between us. Then John hurriedly opened the front door and walked down the steps and out toward the hangar.

On the way, he called in at the store to ask Charlie if he needed anything from Vancouver. There he met the mechanic's wife, who asked him if she could have a ride for herself and her granddaughter. She had been looking after her granddaughter while her daughter was having a baby, and now it was time to take the little girl back to her parents.

"Sure," John grinned. Charlie watched the three of them go out and then disappear inside the hangar.

When John left the house, I went over and sat down on the couch in front of the big window. I didn't look out, but just sat there going over in my mind everything that John would be doing. I didn't have to watch to see him get the Comanche out of the hangar, lift the hood, check things over, open the door and climb in. I had watched him do all this countless times before. And because I had not been looking, I thought John was alone in the plane when it took off.

I could hear the throb of the engine now, so I stood up by the window to watch. I could see the plane, but I couldn't see John. Silently I went through the motions with him as he fastened his seat belt, checked the instruments and taxied down the runway. The engine burst into a roar as the plane sped down the strip. As I watched, the machine lifted off the runway, up over the Chilcotin River, up toward the Davey Allan, Scallon and Wilson Ranches and the Big Ditch. While I looked, I thought of the view that John would have of the ranch every minute of his ascent—the view that I had seen so many times as I sat beside him. I watched until the plane was a tiny speck in the sky. Then suddenly it disappeared into the clouds.

Now that John was away, I shook off my uneasiness. There was just too much to do. I had to get our clothes ready to take back to Williams Lake Sunday night. The beds needed changing and the house needed tidying. Whatever job I tackled I could not seem to put my mind to it. Several times during that long day I found myself on the edge of a chair, immersed in deep thought. Then I would catch myself, get up and move on to another chore.

The three boys and Susan got up, had breakfast and announced they were going out riding.

"Be careful," I told them.

They just grinned and nodded. I was always telling everybody to be careful, and the words didn't have any real meaning anymore.

"Why don't you go and lie down for awhile, you look beat," Doris Minor said as I passed her in the kitchen.

She and her husband, Dode, and Aunt Kathleen were living at the house now so that John would have some company when the kids were away during the week.

I shook my head. "Too much to do," I told her. But I continued to wander aimlessly.

Eventually it was time to help the cook prepare dinner. Our three visitors were going to eat with us and then go right back to Vancouver. As I was setting the table, I thought about each guest as I put his plate slowly into place. This was another habit of mine. I guess it is something you pick up when you are left with your thoughts for long periods of time.

There was Bryce Stringam now. He was a graduate engineer and a Mormon bishop. Just the day before, John had said what a "peach of a guy" he was. Bryce had one of those fresh, happy faces—the kind of face that made you feel good just to look at him.

My son Barry stuck his head in the door. "What time will Dad be home?" he asked.

"At three," I told him.

Susan and Ross came in soon after and they started wandering about the house, not doing anything in particular. Finally, we all ended up in the den.

"What time is it?" asked Susan, going over to the window that looked out on the valley.

"You're much too early," I said. "It's only two."

Nonetheless, I went over and stood beside her, my eyes scanning the sky. Time moved by very slowly. Finally, Ross went over and sat on a couch in front of a small window which looked down on the airstrip. When he left his position, Barry took his place. Then Susan sat there for awhile. We all began to check the window every couple of minutes.

Two-thirty—three o'clock—three-thirty. I began to worry. John always phoned when he was going to be late. In all the seventeen years he had been flying, John never once let us worry about him for long. If he were more than five minutes overdue, the phone would ring and it would be John telling me where he was and when he would be home.

Now the uneasiness which had been lurking in me all day became a burning feeling in the pit of my stomach. He had to arrive within minutes, or there wouldn't be time for our visitors to get back to Vancouver before dark, as planned. John had been away much longer than was necessary to fly to Vancouver, refuel and return.

"Maybe the fellows were late arriving at the airport, and John had to wait for them," I thought hopefully.

The phone rang sharply. I rushed to the office to answer it, but Doris beat me to it. I thought it would be John.

"No she wasn't," Doris said into the phone, and then she paused, "Who's speaking? Hello—hello—hello?"

"That's funny," Doris muttered as she hung up.

"Who was it?" I asked, and my heart began to pound.

"I don't know," she said. "Somebody wanted to find out if you were in the plane with John today. Then they just hung up. They wouldn't say who it was."

In that instant I knew that something terrible had happened. My stomach turned sick. "Oh no," I whispered, "nothing can happen to John. He's such a good pilot. Dear God, please make it something that he can walk away from."

I darted to the phone and frantically placed a long-distance call to Don Clark's wife in Vancouver.

"Joan? It's Gertie Minor calling. Has Don left for the Chilco yet?"

"Yes, a long time ago," she answered. "When John didn't show up, Don, Bryce and Neil decided to drive up there."

"John.... didn't.... show.... up?" I said the words slowly as one speaking in a trance.

"No, he didn't. We figured he was held up on account of weather or something."

"Oh, Joan, Joan," I cried hoarsely. "He left here hours ago!"

"My God, Gertie!" she cried. "Is there anything I can do?"

I let the receiver fall. It crashed back onto the hook of the phone. Now I knew that John was gone. If he had been in his little Super Cub, I told myself, he might have had a chance. But in that powerful Comanche, he couldn't just set down anywhere.

Doris switched on the radio and I screamed, "Turn that thing off." By this time Ross, Barry and Susan had gathered in the office, where I still sat weakly by the telephone. I looked at them silently as they each sat staring sadly at the floor.

"Nothing can happen to him, God, for their sakes. Dear God, don't let it be so. He's too young and he's too good."

Leaving the children sitting there, I walked silently into our bedroom and leaned against the side of the window, staring fixedly down the road. Scenes from various movies came rushing to my mind. There would be a fatal accident and the police would come to tell the family. I knew that someone had to come now, since no one had telephoned. I put my fingers to my temples and prayed, "Dear God, if this had to be, please help me to be strong and brave for my children, that's all I ask." And as I prayed I kept thinking, "Someone is going to come and tell me that he has crashed, but that he is alright. He has to be alright. John couldn't die."

My eye was caught by a movement on the road. It was a black sedan, and it was coming up to the house. The car stopped and a Mountie stepped out. He was followed by a minister. Once more I breathed, "Dear God, help me to be strong, for the children's sake."

I watched as the two men walked up the path and rang the bell. I heard Dode's voice, then I left the bedroom and arrived at the door just as the Mountie was whispering something to him. I sagged against the frame of the door.

"Isn't there any hope at all, Constable," I asked weakly. He shook his head. "No ma'am, I'm afraid not."

In the office, Susan, Barry and Ross started to cry. What can I tell them to ease the pain? I thought. I must not cry—not now.

I went in to them. "Don't cry," I said softly, "It's all right. Dad is safe with God." I took turns holding each of them in my arms, trying to find comforting words.

I looked toward the minister who had followed me in, thinking to myself. "You are a man of God. You should be able to explain why this has happened. Why can't you help us and make the children stop crying?"

As if he read my thoughts, he came over to us.

"Let them cry," he said softly, "that's the best thing for them. Don't try to stop them."

Then little John came in. He had been out with the men. He came to me at once and we held on to one another tightly.

"Be brave," I whispered to him.

There was a catch in his voice as he said, "Don't worry, Mom, we'll be okay."

Then I knew that somehow we would all make it.

David Willness arrived. When we told him what had happened he shook his head, refusing to believe it.

"It's not true," he said hoarsely. "If John crashed, he'd

walk away from it."

For one fleeting moment I grasped at this glimmer of hope. Then I remembered the Mountie's "No ma'am, I'm afraid not."

"Face realities, David," I snapped. "It's all true."

The Mountie joined us. "If I could get hold of the person who phoned to ask you if you were in the plane," he said, "I would hang him."

"I'm glad it happened in that way," I told him. "If I hadn't had a little bit of warning before you came to the door, I think I would've gone to pieces."

Suddenly, I remembered that we had a meal on the stove and automatically headed for the kitchen. On the way, I met, Anna, our cook. She was carrying two large bowls of hot vegetables to the table.

"John crashed," I told her.

Anna screamed and threw the vegetables up into the air. Then she collapsed in a heap on the floor. I looked at her numbly for a second, then stepped over her and continued my journey to the kitchen.

At that moment, Richard Hughes and another fellow came in through the back door. They had heard the news in the yard right after they had arrived down from cow camp where Richard had been working for the past three weeks. Richard had a scared look in his eyes. I walked over and leaned on his shoulder and whispered, "John's gone."

He held on to me and patted my shoulder.

"Yes, I heard," was all he said.

Then I remembered something John had said to me.

"You're a funny one, honey. When some little thing happens you get all upset. But when something big happens, you're as steady as a rock."

"Dear God," I prayed as I headed for the office again. "Let me be as steady as a rock now."

As I walked through the house, the phone was ringing madly and people were coming and going. Little John, Ross, Barry and Susan were all sitting in the office when I got there. I told them to come with me and took them into my bedroom where we could close the door. I told them to be brave so that Dad would be proud of them, and gradually they began to come around. As we talked, we made plans and each one had his say. We all tried to forget about our personal grief and think of each other.

"Are we going back to Williams Lake tonight so we can go to school tomorrow?" Ross asked.

"No," said Little John emphatically.

"I think we should," Barry volunteered. "Dad would just say, 'That's the way the old mop flops' and he would never let anything interfere with what we had to do."

"Oh Barry," I said. "I need you all here with me now. You're all being awfully brave, but I don't really think Dad would expect you to go to school tomorrow."

By bits and pieces the story of John's accident came to us. He had crossed the treacherous Coast Range and was literally in sight of the Vancouver airport on Sea Island when his plane crashed in some trees at Surrey, a rural suburb of Vancouver. He had radioed to the control tower saying he was ten minutes from the airport, then, for some unknown reason the plane had just simply nose-dived to the ground. Perhaps John had a heart attack or had been overcome by fumes. I suppose we will never really know what happened.

At ten o'clock, the partners, Neil Harvie and Bryce Stringam, arrived with Don Clark. They had heard the news on the car radio and said they were surprised to find me so calm and the children asleep in bed. We talked about funeral plans and this gave me an eerie feeling, because I had gone through it all two or three times in my dreams. We decided to have the funeral in Medicine Hat the following Thursday. John would be buried in the family plot beside the bodies of his mother and father, and we would try to get Reverend Taylor, the same minister who had married us, to perform the funeral service.

Bryce Stringam volunteered to look after these arrangements.

As we were talking, the Mountie's wife arrived. She was a nurse and had come to bring me some pills.

"Have you cried today?" she asked.

I shook my head.

"You *must*," she said. "It will make you feel better."

But somehow the tears refused to come. I had not eaten anything since breakfast and I hadn't slept. Suddenly I felt

160

sick. My stomach heaved, but there was nothing in it to come up. I felt sick, cold and dizzy—and very, very tired. In a daze I stumbled up to bed. As I lay there shivering, the "if only's" came to haunt me. If only I had said "no" on those occasions when the decision to move had to be made, things would be different. Things that John had said to me kept passing through my mind.

"Do you love me?" I had teased him one day as we sat in the kitchen.

"Yes," he said seriously.

"How much?" I had challenged.

"Well," he replied slowly, "I'd die for you."

And maybe this is just what he had done, I told myself, in a paroxysm of misery. Then I remembered a time when we had sat reading together and I had said to him, "John, how do you know there is a God?"

"I just know, that's all. And I feel that people would never mourn for a departed one so much if they truly believed in God. The way they conduct funerals today is all wrong. When I die, I hope everybody will square dance at mine," he laughed.

Somehow I felt better after that. And I fell asleep.

When we arrived in Medicine Hat we went to the home of John's sister. Many of John's family were there, and my three sisters, Evelyn, Vivian and Doris, had all come. As soon as I talked to the family I began to feel better. It was such a relief to be surrounded by those who had loved John and to be able to share my loss with them.

Then those forbidding black cars came for us, and we drove to the church. John and I had never believed in mourners processions and here I was now a part of one. I had never believed in a display of human emotions and wondered if the children and I could continue to be calm throughout the service.

As we got out of the car and walked slowly toward the church, I turned and looked at them following me.

"Are we alright?" I asked.

They nodded and I felt more confident.

As we entered the church and started down the aisle, I realized I'd seen this exact scene before in my dream, and at

161

the same time the most peaceful feeling I have ever experienced came over me. It was if a huge weight had suddenly been lifted from my shoulders. When I saw the faces of the mourners, they all seemed so very sad. I wanted to go up to each one of them and say, "Don't be sad. John's life was a good and happy one."

I looked at the pallbearers and remembered something John had said about each one of them. He had loved them all.

And then Rev. Taylor began to speak. It seemed as if only a few days had passed since John and I had stood before him and he pronounced us man and wife, "till death do us part." And now death had parted us and here I was, sitting in front of the same minister who looked a little older, a little grayer as he began his comforting sermon.

It was one of those perfect autumn days, with the warm sunlight spilling through the open windows of the church. I heard the sound of an airplane motor. As I looked out the long window nearest to me, I saw it pass in the sky. And I thought of all the years I had watched a similar plane—one that had brought me joy, sometimes worry, and such a lot of sorrow.

Before I knew it, the service was over. As we moved down the aisle, my son John took my arm. When we reached the top of the steps outside, I turned and looked at him. He smiled and I smiled back. "He is little John no longer," I told myself.

John and Ross accompanied their father's coffin to the graveside, but I took Barry and Susan to the home of a relative. Somehow I did not want the two youngest ones to see their father's body going into the ground.

Later, I worried that people would criticize me for not being at the graveside, so I spoke to Rev. Taylor about it.

"We do what we believe is right to do," he said. "If you have done what you think is right, it doesn't matter what people say."

At the house, we had a few minutes to relax before the crowd arrived from the service. While I was in the bedroom straightening myself up, I heard Susan and Barry in whispered consultation outside the door. Soon they came in and stood quietly looking at me.

"Mom," said Susan, "we'd like you to take off your hat."

I seldom wore a dress hat, but it had seemed the proper thing to do on this occasion.

"Why?" I asked, surprised at their request.

"Because we like you better without it," she said crisply.

This amused me, but I took it off to please them.

At the reception later in the afternoon, we talked to friends we hadn't seen for a long, long time. They asked me what my plans were and I replied with confidence. "I am going to stay at the Chilco. We are just going to carry on as John would have, developing and building the ranch."

During the reception, Richard Hughes came and told me that Charlie had phoned from the ranch earlier that day to say the men were threatening to walk off their jobs in protest over the poor quality of the meals.

"I think I had better take Earle Hansen and get back there as fast as I can."

"Yes, I think you had better," I nodded. "And I will get back as soon as I can."

Already the ranch was reaching out to me, demanding my attention, and leaving me no time to sit and brood.

Chapter XIX:

Picking Up Threads

When we returned to the ranch, we were determined to carry on our work and our personal lives without a long, dismal period of mourning. We didn't believe in it and we knew John didn't either.

I had been able to accept his death as I had hoped I would, believing that death is as natural as being born—it is a part of God's plan, and how one dies is not as important as how one lives. The length of the life is not the important thing, but the quality of life. John had lived a good and happy life. He had lived more in his thirty-six years than many at eighty-six. He had lived every day to the fullest and as if each was to be his last. With these comforting thoughts I continued on with great hope and faith.

"Don't ever lose your sense of humor," my best friend wrote to me shortly after John's death. Rather she should have said, "Don't lose your sanity," for it wasn't until many, many months later that the significance of her words struck home. Then I could look back with humor on the most difficult period of my life.

The first weekend was the beginning of a period which was to continue for several months. They say that advice is cheap, and it sure must be for I got plenty of it. Letters, telegrams and phone calls came pouring in. Wherever I went, friends and acquaintances—even strangers—would take me aside to speak with me in private. Most of these little chit chats contained words of advice on how to live with my sorrow. Some would be about the lives and general trustworthiness of the people who belonged to the Company. What I heard from one source contradicted information received from another.

I had personal problems too. When I smiled some said my smiles were an indication that I felt no loss at John's death. If I didn't, I was feeling sorry for myself. Later on, being a young widow, I found myself in a role I would have gladly discarded. As John had predicted when we were discussing my dream such a short while ago, propositions and proposals began to arrive in great numbers from the most surprising sources. Every association I had with a male was regarded as an affair. I was madly in love with men I had been seen walking with from the house to the corral.

There was no privacy, not even in thought. I was a fish swimming around in a glass bowl up on a mantlepiece where everyone could watch my every move.

The Moccasin Telegraph provided up-to-the-minute reports on my travels, thoughts, and plans. Again and again the rumors found their way back to me and I wept. People I hardly knew would pour out their personal problems, marital unhappiness, insecurities and financial difficulties to me. Some did it to assure me that I was not the first person in the world to experience such unhappiness and to show me how they had worked through problems of their own. For others it was merely a case of 'misery loves company.' I became embroiled in an emotional sea of shared personal problems, distrust and confusion.

Although I kept up a front of calm cheerfulness, the spirit of confidence that I had brought back to the ranch after the funeral was beginning to erode badly. I was a little uncertain of my ability to face what the future might hold—that is, until my old Indian friend, Joe Atkins, arrived.

Joe appeared at the kitchen door Sunday afternoon and asked Anna, our cook, if he could talk with me. When I went out on the back steps to greet him, he pressed my hand between his palms and looked at me through brown eyes that were brimming with tears. "He was a good man," he said, "good man. I'll look after you and Madeline the rest of my life."

Madeline was Joe's wife, and Joe was not particularily noted for taking care of her. In fact, she was pretty good at taking care of herself. But I knew that Joe meant what he said with all his heart and his simple expression of sympathy brought back my courage and faith. I returned to Williams Lake with the children, confident that we could meet whatever came.

To strengthen my courage further came the most welcome letter I had ever received from John's oldest sister Mary. "Do what you think is best," she wrote, "and you will be alright."

All week I stayed in Williams Lake while the children were at school and on weekends we returned to the ranch to work. There I watched with dismay as jealousy and rivalry began to reveal themselves.

Several people who worked at Chilco came to me in Williams Lake one day and asked if I would come out and act as a mediator in the frictions and disputes that kept occurring.

I said, "That's impossible. I have to be here to look after my family."

"We could live in the dorm at school," Susan suggested.

"But you wouldn't be able to come home for weekends," I protested.

"Sure we could," said John. "I can drive us back."

I was proud of my family at that moment—at the way they were rising to meet the situation.

That week I met with members of the Williams Lake School Board about arranging dormitory space for the four of them. Susan, being only twelve, was under age, but a special provision was made for her case. It was arranged that the children would be living in the dorm after the Christmas recess.

A few days before Christmas, I was sitting in the living room in front of the fireplace when John came quietly into the room. As I looked up, I could see that he was worried about something.

"What's the matter?" I asked.

He looked down at the floor, then looked up at me again.

"Mom," he said, "Charlie's got a saddle out in the store. Dad ordered it for you for Christmas and it came today. We didn't know if you still want it. If you like, I'll ask Charlie to send it back."

"Oh I want it, I want it!" I cried, jumping up.

John's face was all smiles. "I'll go and get it," he said and left the room whistling.

Soon all three boys and Susan filed into the room. Leading the procession was John, carrying my new saddle.

"The last Christmas present," I thought sadly, but I smiled cheerfully at my family. After we had finished admiring the saddle, we set it down by the fireplace where it lay throughout the holiday season.

Christmas is the time of joy so we decided to celebrate it in the same old way and keep our sorrow to ourselves. The next afternoon, John, Ross, Barry and Susan and I jumped into the truck, and drove up to Big Creek in search of a Christmas tree. A fire had ravaged this area years before so all the new trees were fresh and green and of a uniform size.

Each of us took an axe and trotted through the woods to see who could select the best tree. Before any choice was felled, the others had to inspect it. And inevitably someone would argue that his tree, which was located just over the hill, was far better than this one and must be inspected before any decision was made. A good deal of banter was passed back and forth. Realizing that this could go on till dark I said, "Let's just get a tree and get out of here!"

In minutes, a tree was in the back of the truck and we began the return trip to the house. As we drove down the road everyone delighted in pointing out trees along the roadside which were better than the one we had cut down.

"Here we are—surrounded by thousands of suitable trees, and we're unable to decide on which one we want," I laughed. "You remember how we used to pick out a tree in Abbey?" Back in our Saskatchewan home there would be a tree stand set up in a vacant lot on a corner somewhere and we usually had about two dozen frozen trees to choose from. But we always seemed to end up well-satisfied.

That evening, we made a big thing out of setting up the tree and decorating it. By the time darkness fell, the job was done and someone had built a fire in the fireplace. When the logs were crackling merrily we shut off the lights in the room, leaving only the sparkling colors of the tree decorations. Then we all sat quietly around the tree, with the yellow glow of the fire flickering across our faces.

Suddenly the telephone rang, shattering our contemplative mood. It was Jim Quigley, the young Nebraskan who had first looked over the Chilco with John. Could he come

167

for Christmas, he wanted to know?

Could he! It would be good for all of us to have him here.

"We'd be glad to have you," I assured him. "Come as soon as you can."

Christmas morning dawned as clear and sparkling cold as Christmas should be. There was no denying the glory of that morning. It set a mood of quiet happiness throughout the house. Jim Quigley would be arriving that evening. Our friends Ross and Helen MacLean had arrived from Calgary the night before. Dode and Doris Minor and their son Donnie were still living in the house with us, which made three more. Then there would be my sister Doris, her husband, Tom Hanna, and their two sons, Cameron and Stewart, who were coming later in the afternoon, and Richard. Only Charlie, the storekeeper, would be missing from our Christmas party. He was away on a well-deserved holiday.

By one o'clock all the gifts had been opened and the mess more or less cleaned up. Filtering in from the kitchen came the delicious aroma of Christmas dinner. I wandered out to the comfortable warm kitchen and sat down to watch Anna work. There she began a subtle campaign of comical antics, comments and stories in an effort to make me laugh. I relaxed under her efforts and my mood mellowed.

Richard and Barry came into the kitchen and sat down and we began to talk. Suddenly we heard a shout, "Fire, fire!" We all jumped and looked out the window to see the store engulfed in smoke and flames. People were running in and out, grabbing what they could. There was a lot of shouting and running for buckets and hoses. Richard dashed out to help.

"My God!" I thought, "this can't be true!" and I felt my legs beginning to buckle. I caught the edge of the window sill and hung on.

Then pandemonium broke loose. It sounded like a shoot-out in a Western movie, as the heat of the flames exploded bullets and burst tins of canned goods. With dismay I thought of all the valuable merchandise being destroyed before my eyes—the expensive riding equipment, guns, clothing and furniture. There was a great roar of flame as the fire reached our supplies of cleaning fluid and paint.

Just at that moment, an Indian ran down the road past our window carrying something from the store. It was a large bag of pink popcorn.

"All those things, and he chose popcorn," said Helen, who had just joined us.

The door opened and her husband Ross MacLean—who was a doctor—staggered through with a reeling Indian. The man had cut his hand while trying to fight the fire. I thought he must be in shock for he struggled to get away from Ross so that he could return to the scene of the fire.

"Lock him in your bedroom," Ross said to me.

With Helen and I on one side and Ross on the other, we managed to shove the resisting man into the bedroom and we sat on him while Ross examined him.

"What's the matter with him?" I asked, after Ross had bandaged a cut which was bleeding profusely.

"Nothing serious," Ross said, with an exhausted grin. "He's just drunk."

Someone ran into the house while we were still attending to the Indian and shouted, "Everybody better clear out of here—the fire is getting near those gas tanks, and they might explode. If they do, this whole house will go up in smoke."

"So now the house is going to burn down," I thought wildly. For a moment I just stood there in the bedroom staring blankly into space.

"Get your coats on," someone ordered.

Helen put her hand on my shoulder and aimed me in the direction of the door. Somehow I managed to get my coat on and went outside to a waiting car. We all drove up the road and stopped at a point where we could look down on the burning store.

"Even if those tanks do blow, we'll be safe up here," Ross assured us.

As we sat there a car drove up behind us and my sister Doris jumped out. She was pale and worried.

"Doris!" I cried, "the store is burning down!"

"To H with the store!" she said, "I thought it was you going up in the smoke!"

By six o'clock the danger was over. The fire had burned the wooden stand under the gas tank almost through in many places, but the firefighters were able to keep the tanks cool enough so the contents did not explode. All that remained of the store was a smouldering heap of twisted iron and charred wood.

"Well, our luck at Chilco doesn't seem to be improving," I said to no one in particular.

Darkness was falling rapidly as we returned home to our overcooked dinner. Everybody was dirty, hungry and exhausted. Our phone was out and the power had been disconnected. We got some candles out of a closet and lit them. Then we placed the dried out and unappetizing food on the table and sat down for our very first Christmas dinner in the magnificient Chilco house.

Someone started to fill his plate.

"Mom," said Susan. "We forgot to say grace."

"You say it," I nodded.

"For what we are about to receive," said Susan, "may we be truly thankful. For Christ's sake, Amen."

The next morning I was in the kitchen alone when two Indians appeared at the door.

"We want some whiskey," one of them mumbled in a low voice.

"I don't have any," I told them shortly.

They persisted in their demands and began shouting at me. And I shouted back, with a vehemence that surprised them—giving vent to feelings that had been pent up for days.

Upstairs in her room, Anna heard the commotion. She grabbed a gilt sword (a relic from her dead husband's collection) from its place on the wall and ran down the stairs and across the room, brandishing the sword in her right hand.

"Get out, get out!" she shouted, charging at the startled pair of intruders. The Indians fled, and I sat down and laughed as I had not laughed in a long while.

Later that day Charlie returned from his holiday and immediately set about to establish a makeshift store in a room over the garage.

A few days later the children were back in Williams Lake at school and my weeks were long and lonesome. On

Fridays I began to watch the road about 3:30 p.m. and would pace back and forth looking out the window. Then I would relax as I caught sight of the familiar Ford Falcon bus churning up clouds of dust as it sped along the ranch road.

The vehicle didn't seem any too safe to me, and I remembered how John had worried about us when we used to make the journey in a heavy station wagon. Now his son—a mere sixteen—was making the trip in this little vehicle which had no real protection in front should he run into a heavy lumber truck. To make matters worse, because most of the Chilco children were attending school in town, John often had as many as thirteen passengers with him, most of them younger than himself.

But every Friday evening, the bus would roar into our yard on schedule, full of singing children. When they pulled up in front of the house, they would all let out a great yell. The door would burst open and they would come charging out, full of laughter and the irrepressible spirit of youth.

Chapter XX:

What Else Can Happen?

My lawyer phoned me from Vancouver to say there would be a business meeting of all the partners late in January.

"You must decide what you want to do," he said. "If you want to continue on with the Chilco Ranch or sell it. You are the majority shareholder and the decision is yours."

"Sell it? Oh, we don't want to do that," I said, "I'm sure we can handle it fine. There's enough good men in the company to keep it going." Although the Moccasin Telegraph had reported that some of the partners wanted to sell immediately, others were as anxious as I was to keep it going. We had to think of all the lives involved, though, especially John's sister Alice and brother-in-law and family at the Abbey Ranch. They had moved to the ranch for good, as we had moved to Chilco, and it would mean drastic changes again for them if Chilco-Abbey was sold.

"If some want out," I said, "maybe the others could buy their shares. All I want is to be fair to everyone and do what's right."

When the company was formed, no provision had been made for the appointment of a successor in the event of John's death. Such a thing didn't seem possible—yet here we were, faced with this "impossible" event.

"If it is sold," my lawyer said, "maybe you would want to buy Abbey back." But I wasn't listening.

"We can't sell Chilco," I said. "We must carry on."

At the meeting there was a general desire on the part of everyone present to carry on with the Chilco Ranch.

Neil Harvie, one of the partners and an experienced Alberta rancher, became our new General Manager, flying out once a month from his ranch near Calgary in his plane, and more often if necessary. Dave Willness, John's brother-in-law, was put in charge of irrigation. Dode Minor, John's cousin was officially put in charge of the cattle.

I automatically became Medical Supervisor, Head of the Department of Grievances and Internal Strife, and also Acting Head of the Worrying Department. And so, with all these important official departments filled, Chilco carried on.

February 13 was my son John's birthday. We decided to hold a special celebration because Tony Minor was being released from his three months in the Williams Lake Hospital. His father, Perry, and his brother, Tad, had driven all the way from Medicine Hat to Williams Lake to get Tony and drive him home for the remainder of his convalescence. But before returning to Alberta, the three of them agreed to come to the ranch and help us celebrate John's birthday. What a happy celebration it was! Tony was so pleased about his release from hospital that he hobbled around the room on his crutches, joking with everybody. The three of them stayed the night with us and prepared to set out for Medicine Hat next morning.

Next day, Tad and his father had a friendly argument about who would drive the car. Tad finally won.

"I don't care who drives just so long as we get there in one piece," said Tony as he settled himself happily in the back seat.

As the car took off down the road, we all waved goodbye. "Good luck," I called after them.

Half an hour later, a neighbor ran breathlessly into the house to say that our recently departed visitors had had a head-on collison with a lumber truck only a few miles from the ranch. The long-feared collision on the treacherous narrow road had occurred at last!

"Oh no!" I cried, after a moment of shocked silence. Then the hot tears began to run down my face. "What else can happen?" I sobbed. "What else can happen in this terrible place?"

Dode rushed over and tried to comfort me. But all I could hear was the screaming in my own mind. Then the sound surfaced and I yelled, "I don't want to stay here any longer! I want to get out of this God-forsaken country! I want to go home!"

Once I had given vent to these words I grew calmer and I realized they had been buried in there wanting to get out all the time. The Chilco dream had turned into a nightmare and I could not stay in this den of tragedy any longer.

"They've been taken into Williams Lake to the hospital," Dode said. "I guess we'd better get in there and see what we can do."

At that so-familiar hospital we entered the emergency wing and sat down in the waiting room with a bunch of other sad-faced people. A nurse came in to tell us that Perry and Tad were only scratched and bruised—the accident had done little more than knock out a few teeth.

"They're being fixed up right now," she said cheerfully, "and they'll be out soon." Then I asked about Tony. "He's in a lot worse shape," she admitted. "His leg is broken again and his jaw is broken. Some of his teeth were knocked out and there are bad cuts around his eyes."

I sat down again numbly, thinking of Tony's happy face and friendly manner, recalling the time he had flown the small plane into Kamloops wondering why so many people were all lined up to greet him as he landed and was whisked away quickly by officials. Tony had taken over the smaller plane to help at cow camp when John bought the "Comanche," and when he was landing at Kamloops, he was almost knocked out of the air as two big turbo-jets came thundering down on him. One of them carried the Duke of Edinburgh.

"And here I thought all those important people were out to greet me!" he laughed later.

The doctor emerged from a room and our eyes met. "You people have really had your share," he said.

"Will he make it?" I asked.

"I don't know. We're going to fly him to Vancouver."

Tony lived, but he did not regain consciousness for two weeks. It was three months before he was able to leave the hospital in Vancouver.

There had been a great build-up of emotion inside me during the months I still clung to the Chilco dream. Now that I had finally decided I could never attain this goal, it

174

was opening the floodgates of a dam. My feelings came pouring out of me. Although I still tried to put on a brave front with my family, I would often break out crying when I was by myself.

About two days after Tony's accident, I was sitting alone in the living room in front of the fireplace with my face buried in my hands when Richard walked quietly into the room. I looked up startled, embarrassed that anyone should see me like this. Then suddenly, this feeling was replaced with a wave of relief. At last I could let someone know how I really felt! I began to talk, and Richard listened quietly as I unloaded my many doubts and fears about returning to Abbey.

"I can't see that we have failed here," I said. "There has just been too much working against us. And yet the thought of returning to Abbey and trying to manage the home ranch scares me."

"After this place, nothing should scare you," Richard commented wryly. "The Abbey place will seem like a breeze."

"I don't really know if I can run that," I told him. "I remember what John used to say about Abbey, 'If you were running this outfit, you'd go crazy.'"

"I'd say you've just about been there and now you're on your way back," Richard said soberly. "But, if you decide to return to Abbey, I'll go too, and I'll stick with you and the kids as long as you need me. I'll do everything I can to help you."

"I have an idea we're going to need you," I said, as I thanked him.

Knowing we would have Richard with us restored a little of my confidence. Now that I had set aside my ambition to master the Chilco, I lost that great drive which had enabled me to carry on each day. I just sat around the house staring into space, hardly eating.

It was Anna who insisted upon knocking holes in the wall of despair I had built around myself. She would bring me trays of attractively-arranged food and would sit across from me, encouraging me to try at least a little bite. She even indulged in comical antics—a non-command performance for an audience of one—until finally I had to smile and then laugh at her. Once I began to laugh, I began to eat.

Chapter XXI:

Going Home

Throughout the following months the wheels were set in motion to sell this Chilco Ranch which had been sold so many times. We had been so sure that we would succeed where the others had failed! One part of me longed to see the place go so I could leave, and the other still retained a wild hope that I might somehow rescue my impossible dream. Before I knew it, it was summer and the children were home for their two-month vacation. And still the big ranch attracted no buyers.

With the lack of definite news, tension mounted among the men. You could feel it in the air. The Chilco floundered like a herd without a lead cow or point rider. Everyone felt that his job was insecure.

Richard did not go to cow camp that summer. He stayed down near the buildings, working at whatever jobs needed doing and watching the family—not because we were afraid of them getting into danger, but because they could easily become prime targets for vented emotion with all the friction that was around. It was a comfort to me to see one pair of friendly eyes among all the unfriendly glances I received as I moved about the ranch.

We had begun to work on the new store as soon as the frost had come out of the ground that spring. By midsummer, it was pretty well complete. The new building was a big improvement over the old frame structure which had served this ranch community for over sixty years. It had much more room and a lunch counter had been added, with Charlie appointing himself chief cook and bottle washer.

Above the store, we had built a couple of suites to accommodate the partners, who often paid a visit to the ranch with their families, and also a room where we would show Saturday night movies.

One bright morning in July, I was wandering listlessly about the house trying to get enough enthusiasm to get outside and go for a ride when the telephone rang. My spirits rose when I heard Bryce Stringam's warm and friendly voice.

"Hello Gertie," he said. "I'm here in Williams Lake with my wife and three daughters. We were wondering if you would have room to put us up if we came out to the Chilco for a few days. The girls have never seen the place."

"You come right ahead!" I cried. "The new store is just finished now and you can have one of the suites. You'll have lots of privacy there and you can stay as long as you want!"

"Good, we'll be right up," he said.

"Quick," I said to Susan, as I hung up the phone. "We're going to have our first visitors in the new suites. That means there are beds to make and cleaning to do."

"Why the big rush?" she said. "They're still over sixty miles away."

In a few minutes we were up in the suite busily sweeping up the sawdust. The new lumber smell was fresh and invigorating. Below us, we could hear Charlie dealing with his customers and the creak of his ladder as he pushed it over to take down some of the merchandise that had been neatly arranged along his new shelves. Even with the additional space, his new store was piled to the ceiling with goods. We could hear him happily singing in his strong tenor voice as he went about his business.

"Hey, Mom, look at this!" cried Susan, as she stared out the window. "Some of the men are drinking it up outside."

"Oh no!" I groaned as I ran over beside her.

Sure enough, leaning against the trees near the road below were several already intoxicated cowboys and Indians with bottles tipped up to their months. Every time they stopped drinking, they would laugh and swear loudly.

"Wouldn't you know they would decide to get drunk today when we have a Morman bishop and his family coming," I said resignedly.

Susan was too busy laughing to pay any heed. Suddenly, I too saw the humor of our predicament. We both doubled up along the wall and laughed until we almost cried.

"But what are we going to do?" I cried.

"Nothing," Susan grinned. "Because there's nothing we can do. They've started their celebration and it has to run its course."

"But why today?" I lamented.

"Why not?" she retorted. "To them, one day is as good as the next."

When Bryce arrived with his wife and daughters, he said nothing about the little show which was still in progress underneath the window of their suite. But I watched his daughters' eyes grow bigger and bigger as they observed the drunken antics of this impromptu troupe. And the show went on until nightfall rang down the final curtain.

Although the local dances of the Cariboo country have become almost legendary, in twelve months there I had never attended one. Knowing this would be my last summer at the Chilco, I decided that I must attend a dance. So, we all decided to take in the big do which was being held after the Riske Creek Rodeo.

The unpainted one-room community hall at Riske Creek was bulging with people when we pulled into the parking lot sometime after ten p.m. But more and more kept crowding in. It reminded me of that chocolate bar ad when the cows keep streaming into a tiny barn and you can't see any coming out at the other end.

A noisy, happy carload of celebrants were passing a bottle back and forth between the front and rear seats of a rusty old pre-war Dodge which sat alongside our stationwagon in the parking lot. I slid over to the far side of our car so as to get out on the opposite side. As we groped our way between the cars toward the rectangle of light that marked the open doorway, we caught the full blast of the music. I peered at the people swinging away inside and wondered how they found room to move. Then, on the other side of the in-going line, I saw there was another line coming out—heading for more liquid refreshment.

We crowded in the door with some other new arrivals and squeezed ourselves into the already packed room. Whirling around to the strains of lively country music was a pretty good cross-section of the Chilcotin country. I could see suntanned cowboys, smiling Indians, their serious-faced women-folk, red-faced businessmen, wide-eyed children and white-faced tourists. Below my feet, the floor vibrated with the stomp of heavy boots. Suddenly, a masculine arm gripped me around the waist and swept me into the crowd.

Around and around we spun, back and forth. I began to feel lighthearted for the first time in many months. I was swept up in the carefree atmosphere of this tiny rustic dancehall—carried by the irresistible lilt of the music created by a foot-tapping fiddler, a broad-smiling guitarist and a swinging accordian player. Light of foot and heart, I danced away the hours.

Over in a corner, two men started a fight. A crowd formed around them to cheer on the hero and boo the villain. We went over to watch. I could see the men were pretty drunk. They began dancing back and forth toward each other, taking wild swings and then slowly ducking to miss the blow.

"It's all swing and no hit," grinned my partner and we both laughed.

Eventually the crowd got tired of this lack of action and started to dance again, leaving the mortal enemies to settle their dispute without a cheering section. These little brawls broke out sporadically throughout the evening and were ignored by most people.

As the liquor consumption increased, the music got wilder and the dancing grew less and less co-ordinated.

Some time after midnight, we heard a loud and enthusiastic cheering coming from somewhere in the middle of the floor. We pushed over there to see what was going on. Through the bobbing heads I could see two native women were fighting. Already, long strands of black hair were flying through the air. Suddenly, one scraped her fingernails down the other's face and the blood oozed. This woman retaliated by grabbing the collar of the other's white blouse and yanking. There was a harsh ripping sound and the victor tossed the garment triumphantly to the floor. But her opponent continued to fight bare breasted.

Shocked, I turned to see where Susan was and saw she was standing right next to me.

179

"What are they fighting about?" she asked, wide-eyed.

"Never mind," I said firmly, "we're getting out of here."

But before we could find a way through the pressing crowd, the fight ended as quickly as it had begun. The music started up again and the dance went merrily on.

"Before you move back to Abbey," a neighbor said to me one day, "you should have a drink in the Alexis Creek beer parlor."

"Not a chance," I laughed. "I've never been in a beer parlor and I don't intend to start now."

But a few weeks later, I found myself being lured into this rustic den of iniquity by four friends who claimed that such an authentic remnant of the wild, wild west just had to be seen to be believed. They placated my fears of instant damnation with a promise that, instead of drinking, I could pass my whole time in this pioneer building absorbing its historical atmosphere.

Some atmosphere! The place smelled strongly of stale smoke, beer and human bodies. As we skirted the four small round tables which filled this doll-sized room, the customers stared at us curiously. I chose the table farthest from the bar and we sat down.

"What'll it be, folks?" said the burly bartender cheerfully.

Each of my four companions ordered two glasses, then the bartender turned his gaze on me. "Same for you, lady?" he asked.

"No thank you," I flushed. "I don't drink."

As I found out, nothing arouses the anger of the bartender in a four-tabled parlor as much as having a non-drinker occupying one of his precious chairs.

"You don't drink!" he bellowed loudly. "Lady, we don't want anybody here that don't drink. You're just taking up space."

Every eye in the room focused on me. I could have crawled out of there on my hands and knees. Instead, I just sat smiling stiffly.

Still grumbling, the bartender stomped off toward the bar. When he returned with draft beer for my companions, he just stared at me icily as he counted out the change. I sat primly in my chair trying to look nonchalant until he moved on to the next table. To hide my embarrassment, every once in a while I would make a comment to the others about the antiques which hung everywhere from ceiling and walls. In the process, my throat got so dry I almost did order a beer. But those years of Presbyterian upbringing chased the thought away as soon as it appeared. Finally, I could stand it no longer.

"Drink up your beer fast so we can get out of here," I whispered to the others.

As I rose to leave, I felt a gentle tap on my shoulder. I looked up quickly into Joe Atkins' smiling eyes.

"You drink?" he asked.

"No," I shook my head.

"You good lady. Don't," he said, patting me gently on the back.

Soon the leaves of the trembling aspen turned to gold and then began to fall away—like my dead hopes for the Chilco. The time had come for us to leave this place where we had known such joy and such sorrow. Now that the decision was made, we were looking forward to the future with faith and determination.

When the day of departure arrived and all was ready, I went back into the empty house for one last look around.

I looked ahead through the spacious hallway toward the door of the office. There John had confidently planned a great program of development for this magnificent ranch. And there I had wept over the systematic destruction of his hopes. Tears began to stream down my face. "I must not let the family see me like this," I told myself, wiping my tears and blowing my nose.

After one last look, I walked slowly toward the big walnut door. For a moment my hands rested on the shiny brass knob and I felt reluctant to go through this doorway and leave my regal existence at the Chilco house behind. But the moment passed, and I slipped out to greet my waiting family with a smile.

Beside the car I paused to take in all I could of the scene around me—the road winding toward the Stone Reservation and beyond to Deer Creek—across the irrigation ditches to the empty hangar at the edge of the huge valley in front—along the road to Lee's Corner and Hanceville—and the ranch buildings nestled against the conifer-crested hill. My last look at Chilco. As we slowly made our way across the valley, heading east toward Saskatchewan and the Great Sandhills, I knew I would never be back to the Cariboo Country again.

Afterword

Neil Harvie, partner and rancher from Cochrane, Alberta, bought three different parts of Chilco. The Cotton, Al Meadows and Deere Creek.

Three years later an auction was held on the ranch where everything went under the hammer, cattle, horses, equipment and land.

The new owner of the ranch was Jim Stewart of Kelowna who later sold it to Vancouver businessman Dick Newsom who resold it to Roger and Harley Hook of Kamloops in 1975.

I dedicate this book to:

...my son John Minor III, his wife Erica, their children Melanie, Tracy and Tammy

...my son, Ross Minor

...my son Barry Minor, his children Cindy, Carrie, Kelly and Marty

...my daughter Susan Skeates, her husband Murray, their children Barkley, Kristy and Brodie

...my daughter Janet Roger

...and my son Gordon Roger.

Printed in USA